# THE STORY OF

# ELDERHOSTEL

# Eugene S. Mills

University of New Hampshire

Published by University Press of New England

Hanover and London

# THE STORY OF
# Elder-
# hostel

UNIVERSITY OF NEW HAMPSHIRE

Published by University Press of New England,

Hanover, New Hampshire 03755

© 1993 by Eugene S. Mills

All rights reserved

Printed in the United States of America  5  4  3  2  1

CIP data appear at the end of the book


Unless otherwise noted, all photographs

© Jim Harrison, whose permission

the author gratefully acknowledges.


Bottom illustration on page iii courtesy

of Elderhostel Canada.

TO DOTTY, DAVID, AND SARA

# CONTENTS

# III. THE THEME

# FOREWORD

When Jimmy and I left the White House in 1981, we faced not only political defeat, but a number of personal crises for which we had not prepared. The end of Jimmy's presidency marked the close of what had been for both of us ten years of full-time careers in political life; now, we wondered what the future could possibly hold for us. Returning to our home in Plains without our now-grown children would be a strange and painful experience. And because of some unforeseen developments in our warehouse business, we faced heavy debt and uncertainty about our financial security.

These difficulties combined to leave us frustrated, sad, anxious, and very worried. Not only were we worried about our future, we worried about what would happen to the country under its new leadership. Would all of our hard work go to waste?

It took many months and some hard searching before we were able to adjust and come to the realization that our experience is one shared by many, if not all, older Americans. While being the First Family of the United States is certainly a unique and privileged occupation—with many benefits as well as complications—what we went through in leaving the White House is common to most individuals who make the transition to retirement, whether involuntary or otherwise.

In our work-oriented society, most of us identify ourselves, and are identified, by our jobs. As children we wonder what we will "be" when we grow up, and it follows that once we end our careers, we cease to "be." Retirement is usually thought of as the end of meaningful life, after which decline and constricting opportunities are the only possibilities.

Living as "retired" people since 1981, Jimmy and I have discovered that the later years need not be limited in any way. Coming to this realization has not been easy or painless, in no small part because we had internalized society's harmful stereotype of older people as unproductive and powerless. But with encouragement from each other and through our involvement in many projects, we have found that retirement can be a time of challenge, growth, and liberation.

As we describe in our book, *Everything to Gain: Making the Most of the Rest of Your Life,* Jimmy and I have spent the last few years pursuing our interests, new and old: teaching, organizing programs and conferences at the Carter Center, traveling, volunteering, working and exercising in the outdoors. I have been especially involved in the struggle to improve mental health care in this country, and in trying to inform the public about issues of health in general.

These activities have added a kind of satisfaction and meaning to our lives that we could not have realized had we still been caught up in the hectic world of career politics. In addition, through these experiences we have become acquainted with countless individuals and organizations whose caring dedication to their work provides us with continuing inspiration.

One of these organizations is Elderhostel, the subject of this book. Jimmy and I first became aware of Elderhostel through the visits to our church in Plains by hostelers attending programs at Georgia Southwestern College (GSW). We were impressed by the enthusiasm of the participants in the program, and by their obvious pleasure as they described the benefits of Elderhostel's combination of study, travel, and friendship.

The director of the local program told us that her goal for each Elderhostel visit is to take the large, diverse group of people who previously had not known each other and to provide them with such an educational and rewarding experience that they will never forget it.

Each activity is designed with this in mind, including a visit to Maranatha Baptist Church to hear Jimmy teach Sunday school, lunch at our historic Windsor Hotel, and extracurricular and on-campus activities involving regular GSW students.

The hostelers tell wonderful stories of visits to the Georgia coast to watch the sea turtles emerge from the sea and lay their eggs at night; of traveling to Andersonville National Historic Cemetery in our county, where many have looked up and found relatives who were prisoners there during the Civil War.

One man wanted a game set up for him with the tennis pro at the college. The director gladly fulfilled his request, thinking "the poor guy will be worn out when the pro gets through with him." Not so—the Elderhosteler beat the pro.

The oldest person (thus far!) who has come to one of the GSW programs was a woman, ninety-four years old. She listened to one of the professors at the college perform a monologue of Will Rogers and then told the audience that when she was fifteen her parents had taken her to see Will Rogers in person. She was an instant celebrity.

One particular Elderhostel group insisted on providing the entertainment for the director of the program at the farewell banquet, instead of vice versa. They wrote a script and produced a play. They were the actors and actresses, using their own talents, singing and playing the piano, dancing and joke-telling. It was the hit of all banquets and was inspired by an acting class they had during the visit to the college.

Elderhostel helps break down the barriers and stereotypes associated with old age. By giving citizens over sixty access to colleges and universities—traditionally the realm of the young—it proves that older people can continue to be adventurous and productive. The program proves this to society, and more importantly, to the older participants themselves.

*The Story of Elderhostel* is the story of these participants—hundreds of thousands of them—who are making the same transition to "life after work" that Jimmy and I made when we left Washington. In the pages that follow, you will meet many of them, each of whom has his or her own inspirational story to tell. The readjustment process they describe is never easy, but thanks to Elderhostel, it is a great deal easier for a great number of people.

In my efforts over the years to improve the mental and physical health of people, I have learned that not just those afflicted by disease, but *all* of us, must take active measures to remain as healthy as possible. Elderhostel contributes directly to the health of its participants—and by extension to all of us who witness their example—precisely because it is active; it allows older people to be involved and engaged, to "make the most of their lives"—and, of course, to have fun!

Consider *The Story of Elderhostel* part of your essential health care routine. Reading it will be some of the sweetest medicine you have ever taken.

Rosalynn Carter

# PREFACE

It has been my good fortune to be associated with Elderhostel since its founding days at the University of New Hampshire. As president of the University, as an Elderhostel board member, and finally as chairman of the board, I have been involved in much of the life of the organization and have known most of those who have played major roles in its growth. It also has been my privilege to know many Elderhostelers and to visit programs in this country and abroad; my wife and I have participated a number of times.

In my conversations with hundreds of hostelers I have been struck by their curiosity about the origins and the development of *their* program; moreover, it has been clear that many participants have only vague or even incorrect views about the organization. I have heard hostelers tell colleagues that the program was founded at Stanford University, that it is partially financed by the federal government, that on occasion the massive mailing list is sold to commercial organizations, and that Elderhostel was created specifically to provide college opportunity for senior citizens who had never been to college. Each of these statements is false.

Although it has seemed evident that telling the story of Elderhostel would be helpful to hostelers and to others who are interested in this remarkable organization, my motivation to write a book was in large part an expression of my respect and admiration for the participants. They are wonderfully attractive and stimulating people. The story of

*Preface*

Elderhostel is basically a story of hostelers and their enthusiastic teachers. But it is also a story of organizational growth, leadership, and international cooperation.

It is a pleasure to acknowledge those who have been of special assistance in writing this book. President William D. Berkeley and Vice-President Michael Zoob have been generous in time and counsel and have read the manuscript. Former Canadian Elderhostel Board Chairman Walter Pitman, and Executive Director Robert H. Williston, have been available for consultation; the latter made a number of suggestions concerning Chapter 7. James Verschueren, director of the Elderhostel Institute Network, read Chapter 13 and provided advice.

Founders Martin P. Knowlton and David Bianco were, as always, candid and informative, especially with respect to the early history of the organization. Their cooperation was essential to the project and I am grateful for their assistance. Board member Merrell M. Clark provided a useful written summary of a number of important points. I also am grateful to Susan W. Nissim and George Tsilides of International Study Tours, and Linda Paxon of Saga Folkestone for their assistance in arranging an extensive foreign trip that made it possible for my wife and me to visit certain programs abroad.

I want especially to acknowledge the assistance of board member Dr. Harry R. Moody. Dr. Moody, deputy director of the Brookdale Center on Aging of Hunter College, read the entire manuscript in an early version and offered a number of extremely helpful comments. His knowledge of Elderhostel and issues related to aging resulted in substantial improvements. I am, of course, entirely responsible for the final product.

Raymond L. Erickson and David W. Ellis have been helpful colleagues throughout this project and I thank them for their friendship and support.

It is a pleasure to acknowledge the excellent editorial assistance of Michael F. Lowenthal, who made important contributions to the manuscript. His literary and editorial skills are much appreciated.

I want also to acknowledge the interest and support of the Board of Directors of Elderhostel. The board members, collectively and individually, have believed in the importance of this book. I hope that it meets their high standards. I thank also Elderhostel staff members, Anne Maida, Karyn Franzen and Cady Goldfield, for unfailing assistance. Jane Angel was helpful in managing the word processing that was required in later versions.

Finally, I thank my wife, Dorothy Mills, for her critical reading of the manuscript and for helpful, independent note-taking during our visits at programs in the United States and abroad. She has shared it all with me—the travels and the notes.

*Tustin, California*                                                    E. S. M.
*June 1992*

At Colonial Williamsburg, a "living museum" of re-created history in Virginia, Elderhostelers learn how authentic eighteenth-century costumes are made. (Photo by Tom Green, Colonial Williamsburg staff photographer)

# THE STORY OF
# ELDERHOSTEL

# INTRODUCTION

The American spirit, from pioneer days through the Industrial Revolution and up to recent times, has been centered on a number of values, assumed by most people to give greater purpose to life. Our national character is inextricably linked with goals of activity, growth, personal advancement, material accumulation, and the development of power. Success, health, upward mobility, sexual activity, and personal independence—all of these are essential components in defining enviable membership in American society.

Perhaps it goes without saying, then, that envy has not traditionally been directed at older people. They may be loved, admired, appreciated, and occasionally even listened to, but rarely envied.

Throughout most of this century, elders were considered to be a problem, a social liability, and an embarrassment. Limits, deterioration, and dependency were widely assumed to be the final outcomes of life. It was believed that the best older people could expect was to achieve retirement (that is, a withdrawal from the essential and productive functions of living) and, surrounded by loving and attentive family members, listen to the radio, watch television (once this became available), and if they were really fortunate, ride their very own lawn mowers into the Great Beyond. All of this was supposed to happen, as a frustrated elder once put it, "while continuing to adore wistfully our youth-oriented culture. In other words, appreciate but don't get in the way." *

As late as 1975, when Elderhostel offered its first programs, American society was only beginning to understand the dimensions of the problems associated with the rapidly increasing older population. Certainly, the general view of the situation was much the same as it had been throughout the earlier decades of this century: older people were supposed to wait out their dwindling and failing years with diminished hopes, reduced ambitions and interests, and loss of the capacity to learn. Late adulthood was truly a grim prospect, often made more depressing by the absence of economic support, inadequate health care, and the loss of opportunity for self-renewal. The assumption that elders would face mental and physical constraints in their later years was constantly reinforced by the accepted view that youth, with its energy, optimism, and ready capacity to learn, was the controlling model for life.

At the same time, there was a surprising discovery about the elderly and their role in the general population: America was growing steadily and irreversibly older. First demographers, and then the general public, began referring to "the graying of America." The rapid growth of the older population was not simply a matter of lengthened life spans brought by improvements to medicine and its technology. As Jerome Avorn has pointed out, the changed population pyramid is based on "The alarmingly straightforward observation that . . . one cannot live to become sixty-five if one has not lived to become ten."[1] Even while acknowledging the importance of improved medical care and biomedical factors, he stresses the "social interventions" that deserve credit for helping to reduce earlier mortality rates: better nutrition, uncontaminated water, and improved housing and sanitation.

The "discovery" of America's aging population led to a variety of unpleasant revelations: nursing home scandals, poverty of such magnitude as to force some older people to eat dog food, the potential bankruptcy of the Social Security system, and the grave health care and

*Unless otherwise evident from the surrounding text, most quotations throughout the book for which no citation is provided have been obtained from: (1) the author's interviews with hostelers and Elderhostel staff, (2) written reminiscences and/or letters provided to the writer, or (3) materials on file in the Elderhostel offices in Boston and Kingston, Ontario.

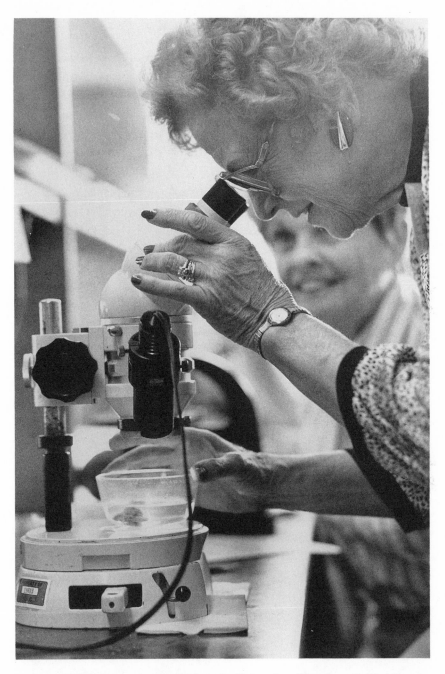

Investigating microscopic marine life at the University of Southern California program on Santa Catalina Island.

economic problems that might follow as a result. It became more and more apparent that the common view of old age as a wasted, tragic time was a self-fulfilling prophecy. As a society we slowly began to realize that the freedom and prosperity we considered so much a part of the American dream were tarnished by our mistreatment and abandonment of older citizens.

The increased awareness of the plight of elders prompted the development of a new view of aging in America, representing a radical departure from the previously accepted notions. In his 1975 book, *Why Survive? Being Old in America*, Robert N. Butler was one of the first people to combat "the contemporary devalued view of older persons" which he had labeled "ageism." Reacting against "prejudice, derogation, discrimination, and stereotyping by younger groups," Butler proposed a new, positive vision, which he termed "a more balanced view of old age." He concluded that older people are diverse; that the overwhelming majority live independently, not in institutions; that "old age" and "brain damage" do not alone bring about changes in older people; that older people are more reflective than impulsive; and that:

The old continue to learn and change in response to their experiences and human relationships. They are not often overwhelmed by new ideas for they recognize how few of them there are. Many are employable, productive, and creative. Many wish to leave their mark through sponsoring the young as well as through ideas and institutions.[2]

Clearly, this new view of older Americans demanded new approaches in social and educational services for elders. Observing that the "wasteful, tragic process of disengagement will continue to grow unless older people themselves can realize their worth and become their own agents of change," Martin P. Knowlton sought ways to make that self-realization a possibility for elders.[3] Long a social and educational innovator, Knowlton joined forces with his friend and colleague David Bianco, and in 1975 Elderhostel was born.

Knowlton conceived Elderhostel as an attack on a society that "cannibalizes the vital years and casts the remainder aside as garbage." Inspired by the adventuresome spirit fostered by European youth hostels,

Nutritious meals—often prepared with a creative flair—are part of the Elderhostel experience.

he and Bianco designed integrated study programs to combat the helpless resentment caused by elders' disengagement from society. The idea was to get elders directly involved with interesting activities and with each other. As the introduction in every Elderhostel catalog explains:

Elderhostel is an educational program for older adults who want to continue to expand their horizons and to develop new interests and enthusiasm. We're for elder citizens on the move, not just in terms of travel, but in terms of intellectual activity as well. Our commitment is to the belief that retirement does not represent an end to significant activity for older adults but a new beginning filled with opportunities and challenges.

The Elderhostel plan combines the excitement and challenge of travel with the enrichment of courses on substantive subjects, taught by highly-qualified teachers. One-, two-, or three-week programs bring together groups of fifteen to forty people over the age of sixty at a college campus, conference center, or retreat. Elders take three noncredit courses accompanied by field trips, extracurricular events, and ample time for socialization. The courses do not carry college credit, there are no tests, and the intent is that students delve into the subject matter for the sheer joy of learning. As one hosteler remarked, "I don't have to study these courses to get a better job or a raise—I don't have a job anymore. I can just study and talk with my classmates for the fun of it."

Elderhostel came along just in time. Harry R. Moody has written, "In retrospect, Elderhostel seems obvious. Elderhostel was not an idea whose time had come but rather an idea that was long overdue."[4] From the beginning, the program contained ingredients for success. It was inexpensive, uncomplicated, and highly accessible, promising lively interaction with peers and, in many cases, interesting travel opportunities. Moreover, the courses that were offered were academically respectable. Elderhostel was a nontraditional program that spoke directly to the needs, interests, and abilities of older citizens.

The success of Elderhostel demonstrates the power of an idea that is favorably timed and creatively implemented. Since 1975, the program has grown from an enrollment of 220 in New Hampshire to a worldwide organization with over 236,000 participant-weeks annually in fifty countries—more than a thousandfold increase in sixteen years! Over half a million people currently receive the Elderhostel catalogs describing course offerings and travel arrangements. This vast company of elders includes approximately 300,000 "alumni"—former participants who, with surprisingly few exceptions, will enroll again in a domestic or foreign program. They are an ever-growing group of people who share an enthusiasm for Elderhostel and a keen appetite for life.

The hundreds of thousands of Elderhostelers in programs around the world reflect a positive, motivated, participatory attitude that is a direct refutation of the American myth of the "used-up elderly." In every program one encounters people who want more out of later life than would ever have been thought possible one or two generations ago. Rather than accepting relegation to the depression and isolation of the leftover years, these elders are engaged: *they are there because they like what they are doing.*

Perhaps most inspiring is that the participants consider their activities to be perfectly natural for older persons. As one hosteler commented, "I don't know why everyone gets so embarrassed and depressed about getting older. My God, I've had more fun in my sixties than in any other decade of my life."

The story of Elderhostel is in reality many stories, each of which could fill a different book. The dramatic success of the organization— its rapid transformation from a two-man show on a shoestring budget to a multimillion dollar international program—could easily make an exciting case study for an organizational historian. Even more interesting, perhaps, would be a scholarly study of Elderhostel's role in educational gerontology, discussing issues such as ageism and lifelong learning in far more depth than the brief treatment they receive in this book.

Another story that might be warranted would tell of those people Elderhostel does *not* reach, and why. It is important to bear in mind that the context for development of Elderhostel included the knowledge that a great number of elders are not likely candidates for enrollment because of poor health, the ravages of aging, poverty, or limited education. Even among those whose financial resources and strong educational backgrounds make them likely candidates for the program, Elderhostel may not always have appeal.

I have chosen here to tell a more personal version of the story, leaving the organizational, educational, and sociological studies to experts in those fields. This book features Elderhostel's people: the key players in its founding and history, the staff members who keep the organization running smoothly, the teachers and program coordinators, and most important, of course, the hostelers themselves. This is the story of Elderhostel that I know best, and the one I believe will be of most interest to the thousands of individuals in the present and future Elderhostel family. As anybody who has been involved with the organization knows, it is truly the people who make Elderhostel what it is.

I have divided *The Story of Elderhostel* into the traditional narrative components of plot, characters, and theme. Keeping in mind the vital importance of participants enrolled in actual programs, we begin not with details of the organization's early history, but rather inside the Elderhostel experience. I hope Elderhostel "alumni" will recognize in the sketches in Chapter 1 something of their own experiences; for those who have not yet taken part in Elderhostel, the sketches should provide a helpful introduction to the reality of the programs.

Chapter 2 introduces the two key players in the founding of Elderhostel, Marty Knowlton and David Bianco. Chapters 3 through 8 feature the history and growth of the organization, from the first summer, through the period of rapid expansion, to the present. Chapters 9, 10, and 11—the "characters" section—present composite profiles of Elderhostel participants, as well as statements by hostelers, instructors, and staff regarding their own Elderhostel experiences. Chapter 12 introduces "the theme" by discussing the philosophy of Elderhostel in relation to the social context for elders in America and the demographics of Elderhostel participants. Chapter 13 is an explanation of the newest initiative, Elderhostel's leadership of the Institute Movement. The final chapter contains reflections upon the success of the organization and the role that it plays in American society.

PART I

# The
# Plot

# CHAPTER ONE

# PROLOGUE: INSIDE THE ELDERHOSTEL EXPERIENCE

## ARIZONA: "GETTING TO KNOW YOU"

A small group of elders clusters together outside the auditorium, still tingling with the sounds of Yehudi Menuhin and the English String Orchestra. The custodians have shut off the lights and locked the doors with alarming speed, and we huddle together against the night air, waiting for our van. This is Arizona, but it is winter, and it is cold. We are all alone.

"Help, we're lost!" somebody calls out. "It's freezing out here."

"Bunch up closer," another says. "At our age we've bunched up with people before."

"But with only one person at a time, right?"

There is laughter and a rustling of jackets as we move together. "Closer," urges one woman, "I need more heat." Someone in the middle responds, "Don't be selfish, I'm already giving you all I've got."

As we press together, tighter and tighter, the chattering of teeth gradually gives way to smiles. The accumulation of body heat allows us all to relax and appreciate the irony of the situation.

"Here we are in the Arizona desert," says the woman who ordered us to bunch closer. "They'll find us tomorrow, frozen in a clump like this. Probably put in a pool all around us and just leave us standing here—a monument to Elderhostel."

Then somebody in the front shouts, "Here comes the van!"

"Ah, too bad," laments one man. "I was just starting to enjoy being so close to all of you. Let's do this again tomorrow night!"

Luckily, we will be able to do it again, because there are several nights remaining in our Elderhostel week at Arizona State University. And if a group of strangers can feel this close after so short a time, we're sure to be best of friends by the end of the week.

It is Sunday, the first day of the program, and after dinner in the Memorial Union Building we have gathered for our first group meeting. An orientation session is the only thing scheduled for this evening, and then we'll return to the motel on the edge of the campus where earlier we found our assigned rooms. Carolyn Salinas and Louise Gibbs, who will handle all our arrangements for the week, pass out schedules, class materials, and maps to help us find our way around the sprawling campus of 44,000 students. After a quick question-and-answer session, we go around the room, to "rise and share."

There are forty-one of us from across the continental United States, all over the age of sixty. We are teachers, homemakers, accountants, a farmer, a research scientist, a foundry worker, and a government administrator. For some, this is a new experience, but when Floyd, a retired architect from Indianapolis, went to an Elderhostel week several years ago he liked it so much he decided to go to one in each state. So far he has been to forty-six programs in thirty-eight states. "It's sort of like deciding to climb all of the mountains in a range that are over 5,000 feet," he says. "I do it because they're there."

Sidney and Selma of York, Pennsylvania, report that he is an attorney and she is a cable-television producer, and that they have frequently been hosts for the popular Elderhostel programs in Ashland, Oregon, centered around the local Shakespeare festival.

Florence of Kirkwood, Missouri tells of her activities: art museum docent, river rafting, sailing, international bicycling, gardening, bridge, and mountain music. After this program she will be leaving for an Elderhostel bike trip in Holland. "A nice, level country," she adds with a smile.

One hosteler gives her occupation as "career volunteer," and several others respond immediately that the designation is appropriate for them as well.

This is clearly a group with an enormous wealth of experiences. It's going to be a lively week.

The next morning at 8:30 is our first class, back in the Memorial Union Building. We file into the conference room with our *Webster's Collegiates* in hand, wondering just how much "Fun With the Dictionary" it is truly possible to have, as our course title would suggest.

Quite a bit, it is clear, as soon as we meet our instructor, Dr. J. J. Lamberts, professor emeritus of English at ASU. A specialist in grammar, philology, and lexicography, he knows how to do just about anything with words. Dr. Lamberts is an old pro, having already taught eighteen Elderhostel classes, and his love of telling others about "this crazy dictionary business" is infectious.

Using dictionaries is second nature for everybody in the class, but for most of us this is the first time we've really thought about the incredible amount of work that goes into the tomes. Dr. Lamberts tells us that producing a modern dictionary normally takes at least $10,000,000 of "front money." The hardest step in publishing a dictionary is not defining the words, as most of us guess, but rather gathering citations, the sentences or paragraphs that demonstrate appropriate word usage.

For the rest of the hour Dr. Lamberts guides us through his ten-page outline of questions and examples, urging us on as we examine word meaning, pronunciation, hyphenation, etymology, synonyms and antonyms, and slang. By the end of the class we have developed a new appreciation of the dictionary: it tells us what the status of the language is, not what it ought to be. Dr. Lamberts brings the point home with a joke: "A purist is a person who gets his information from an out-of-date dictionary."

"But don't be discouraged," he adds as a final note. "Our language has already been 'crupted."

Break time is 9:30 and the coffee flows as freely as the debates between class members. It seems that no matter who you are, language touches close to home, and just about everyone has something to say. Before we realize, it's 9:45—time for the second class.

In coordination with a statewide tribute entitled "Arizona Celebrates Frank Lloyd Wright, 1990–1991," Dr. Josephine Harris will educate us on "Frank Lloyd Wright: The Man, The Myth, The Masterworks." Dr. Harris, a former dean at the California Institute of the Arts, has taught at universities all over the country, and she assures us that Arizona is the ideal setting for a course such as this because Wright's western headquarters, Taliesin West, is here. It still administers the educational programs of the Frank Lloyd Wright Foundation, an organization which preserves Wright's materials and serves as the base for an architectural firm that continues his creative tradition.

Dr. Harris intrigues us with tales of the colorful life of this artist, architect, engineer, and flamboyant genius. Some of the stories seem straight out of the supermarket tabloids, but it's impossible not to be impressed by Wright's achievements. Dr. Harris has selected slides from her immense collection to prepare us for the upcoming field trip. We are shown the Robie House ("a perfect statement of the prairie house"); Hollyhawk House ("so uncomfortable that its owner went to live elsewhere"); the Johnson Building ("beautiful, but now largely unused because of its lack of air-conditioning, narrow stairway, and an elevator that holds only two people"); and the beautiful, memorable Kaufman House, known as "Falling Water."

Telling us when and where to meet for the afternoon's field trip, Dr. Harris releases us for another fifteen-minute recess before our 11:00 class, "Introduction to Arizona: Mining History, Ghost Towns, and Lost Treasures." Our instructor is Marshall Trimble: social historian, author, master of the twelve-string guitar, and working cowboy. "Just-call-me Marshall" was raised in a small railroad town in northern Arizona and he has made a life's work out of his prideful interest in the people of his state.

During the course of his work, Marshall has interviewed cowboys, prospectors, and even a few of the West's most famous madames. He delights in recounting the stories they told him, stories about life in such forgettable towns as Lousy Gulch, Total Wreck, and Why. He urges us to imagine their lives—full of heat and dust, "hairy banknotes" (cattle), liquor, mines, rival Indians and Mexicans—and to appreciate the hardships that were daily trials, especially for the women. Both the promise and the heartbreak are reflected in the words of one unsuccessful miner: "We didn't find the treasure we sought, but we sure found a good place to look for it."

Agreeing with the miner about the attributes of this beautiful state, the class heads out into the midday Arizona sun to get some much-needed lunch. When we've had our fill, it's time to see some of Frank Lloyd Wright's masterworks in person. First stop is the Arizona Biltmore Hotel, an impressive building with which Wright was associated, though one of his former students is considered to have been the principal architect. Next we visit Taliesin West, examining Wright's headquarters in light of the details of his personal history we now know. Finally, we travel to a small house Wright designed in Phoenix. It is attractive, but surprisingly limited, featuring a tiny stairway that is inconvenient for even one person at a time. One hosteler speaks for most of us when he says, "I appreciate Wright's talent much more now, but I still wouldn't want to live in one of his creations."

Back on campus, we have some free time before dinner. Some people read, some swim, others nap or get to know their classmates better. The evening's activity is a movie and the group of us who were stranded after the concert make plans to meet again for the film. With luck, we'll be stranded longer this time.

On the final night we all go to a local restaurant for a special graduation dinner. Each hosteler is awarded a "graduation Certificate" amid much laughter, applause, jokes, and reminiscences about the week.

In the morning everybody is reluctant to leave. It seems as if the week has just begun. Gradually, we say good-bye to each other as we depart for home, or as is the case for many, another Elderhostel program. Lillian of Aurora, Colorado captures the bittersweet mood perfectly when she says, "It's sad to think that I may never see you again,"

Pausing for a smile at the Old Sturbridge Village living museum in Massachusetts.

then adds brightly, "But of course I will. Where are you going to go next year?"

## NEW YORK

### Part I: "Fun is Fun, Too"

"Ten years ago there wouldn't even have been a class on women playwrights," says the instructor, Carol Bellini-Sharp, introducing "Women of the 8os: Two Views From Current Theater." Just as sure, ten years ago the three older women in the front of the room would never have imagined that they would be participating in such a class—and certainly not that they would be about to act out a scene by a radical feminist playwright.

We are at Hamilton College in Clinton, New York, and the play in front of us is Caryl Churchill's *Top Girls*. Scripts in hand, the three hostelers begin the awkward but engrossing task of reading their parts. They play women from different times in history, having lunch with the owner of a temp-secretarial placement service. The performance goes surprisingly well considering it is completely unrehearsed, and there are only a few glitches: "Wait, it's my turn!" "No, we're supposed to speak at the same time." "Oh, I'm sorry. Was that my line?"

The class of thirty-three women and sixteen men shout encouragement and applaud heartily when the scene is done. Since we are all over sixty, we represent a generation that grew up without feminist theory or a national focus on women's rights. Nonetheless, everyone in the class is eager to meet Bellini-Sharp's challenge to consider the contemporary contexts in the development of "a voice for women." Women and men alike are receptive to the issues Churchill's play raises; many of us picked this Elderhostel program precisely because these issues would be a focus point of our week.

Bellini-Sharp highlights the themes of the play, centering on the all-female cast's "sometimes suffocating dependence upon men." In the discussion that ensues, it is obvious that many of the characters' strengths and vulnerabilities are familiar to the women in the class. Both women and men speak to the often volatile issues from personal experience, candidly grappling with questions of real substance: masculine control of the standards for writing; the political, economic, and vocational limits within which women have been forced to live; the double standard for compensation; the need for male sensitivity concerning behavior that is derogatory towards women; and the need for frank discussion of women's concerns.

This is serious stuff, but it is hardly a grim or angry proceeding. The discussion is sparked by good humor and open questioning of other viewpoints. For many of these late-life learners, the ground being broken here is new. One male hosteler said after class: "This has been a real eye-opener for me. I think I now understand what this is all about. I couldn't have said so when I arrived here on campus. I had some major reservations that now have disappeared."

"Well," responded one of the women in the class, "It sometimes takes a long time—too long—to open a window."

Our second class is an exploration of "The Educational Crisis." We are led by Hamilton political science professor David Paris, who we learn is also vice-president of the Clinton Board of Education. Obviously, his approach will be more than theoretical.

Paris begins the first class by quoting the 1983 report of the National Commission on Excellence in Education: "If an unfriendly foreign power had attempted to impose on America the mediocre educational performance that exists today, we might well have viewed it as an act of war." He could hardly have picked a more provocative opening. To a group who were largely college-aged when America's now-educational (and economic) competitor Japan waged actual military war, the statement resounds with implications. This is a class of people deeply concerned about education—former school teachers, corporate executives, community leaders. It is quite a feat that Paris keeps the discussion orderly.

We consider the three "I"s (ideology, interests, and institutions); the history of public education in America; the comprehensive high school; progressive education; the battle over vocational education; ethnic and racial access; and the debate over moral education. Admonishing the class to avoid "PGO"—the penetrating glimpse of the obvious—Paris suggests we try to be constructive in our criticisms of schools. Here is where the practical end of his work starts to show; it is clear this man deals with the realities of schooling, not simply nebulous goals or ideals. It is one thing to indict education, Paris tells us, but it is quite another, a more difficult thing, to help improve schools.

One hosteler agrees, observing almost guiltily, "We expect too much of our schools. Every time the public or government thinks we face a big question—whether it's drugs, economic competition with Japan, the breakdown of the family, or sex education—they say immediately: 'Let the schools do it,' or 'What's wrong with our schools?'"

Paris picks up on the hosteler's point, describing the way society goes through "cycles of crisis and reform, hope and disappointment" with regard to public education. We demand so much of our schools, he concludes pessimistically, that "they are probably doomed to remain in crisis."

After two hours of intense discussion of women's issues and public education, the group welcomes the relief of the next class, "Shakespeare's Comedies." Most of us studied Shakespeare long ago, in college or even in high school, but this is an opportunity to examine the plays without the pressure of tests or memorized speeches. Instead, we will read *A Midsummer Night's Dream*, *As You Like It*, and *Measure for Measure* simply for pleasure, thinking through the origins of the plays, the cultural and political life that they reflect, and the often subtle humor by which they are characterized.

Our instructor, Nathaniel Strout, has barely begun his lecture before a hosteler asks the inevitable question, "Who was Shakespeare? There is always talk that someone else, maybe a prominent person of that time, actually wrote the plays." Strout replies with great seriousness, "My own view is that it wasn't Shakespeare who wrote the plays. They were done by another person of the same name." So much for that burning literary question.

Under Strout's guidance we consider the great and important themes of these great and important plays: choice and fate, belief and cynicism, mercy and mortality, justice and love. The plays provide a window on the life and manners of the sixteenth and early seventeenth centuries and allow us, through contrast, to look at the way we live now. It is a tribute to Bellini-Sharp that some of the discussion focuses on the treatment of women in *A Midsummer Night's Dream*.

Life at Hamilton is not all work and no play. The campus is almost distractingly beautiful and we have ample opportunity for walks, swimming, shopping, and numerous field trips to local attractions such as the Munson-Williams-Proctor Institute and the F. X. Matt Brewery, both in Utica. The Elderhostel coordinator, Gil Adams and his friends Al and Felicia Delucia, add their local commentary at every stop along the way.

On Monday night we take a break with a big group square dance. Everybody gets caught up in the music and the movement, trying to meet the challenge of doing what the caller says when she says it. Hostelers who haven't danced in years are letting go, laughing at their mistakes and even improvising when a lull allows. When one woman sits down for a rest she observes, "I never dreamed I'd be square dancing in my eighties!"

Women and men who a few hours ago were debating the feminist implications of Shakespeare, now dance and laugh together. The moment captures the essence of our Elderhostel week at Hamilton. After all, in the words of one hosteler who calls out in the middle of an allemande left, "Learning is fun, but fun is fun, too!"

*Part II: "Walking on Water"*

Paul Smith's College is situated on the shore of Lower St. Regis Lake, deep in the Adirondacks of New York. The college owns 15,000 acres of wilderness, and it is not surprising that the rural location sets the tone for life at the college: academic emphasis is on environmental issues; personal relationships are direct and uncomplicated; and the goals the college tries to instill are independence, responsibility, and work. The immediacy of the outdoors and environmental concerns is also reflected in the roster of our Elderhostel courses here: "You Are What You Drink: A Water Quality Sampler," "Know Your Needles: Conifer Identification for the Layman," and "Heart Smart Cuisine."

Our group would seem to be a typical mix. Marjorie is a photographer from St. Paul; Loretta from Massachusetts has been to twenty-seven Elderhostels and is well-informed about programs; Geraldine is a retired school teacher from Pennsylvania; Lucille from New York has been involved in gerontology and is here with her husband Bill, who raves about the Elderhostel program they've just completed on Maryland's eastern shore.

As we gather for the first time, our conversation reveals that we are a bunch of "nature freaks": "I'm into birding"; "I love to hike in the woods"; "As far as I'm concerned, if we don't fix this acid rain problem, we're all in deep trouble"; "A college course in biology had a very big impact on my life"; "I get a kick out of taking pictures of flowers and showing them to people in nursing homes." We had all been undaunted by program director Deborah Wells's letter of warning a few weeks earlier: ". . . remember that you are going to be in the mountains . . . bring a pair of sturdy walking shoes . . . a flashlight will come in handy . . . a first aid kit is recommended . . . don't forget to bring insect repellent. Black flies and mosquitoes abound in June." This is the kind of stuff our group thrives on. It's all a part of life in the Adirondacks.

We start off with Chef Sorgule's course. We're a very health-conscious, nutritionally-sensitive bunch, and the chef's tips on how to cook and eat right are much appreciated. Of course, there's the added bonus of eating the homework! But good food isn't enough to keep this group indoors. We're itching to get out and explore this great wilderness preserve of 6,000,000 acres.

Instructor Robert McAleese leads us on our first trip into the field. McAleese "talks trees" along the Barnum Brook Trail with the class strung out behind him, an Adirondack Pied Piper. We have seen a lot of trees in our lives—the thirty-eight of us have, combined, almost 2,500 years of life experience—but McAleese's expert commentary makes us see the forest as if for the first time.

The Elderhostelers can't get enough. Through the week we go on bird walks, accompany "Director Deb" on a canoe trip, and generally revel in the vast teeming world that surrounds "the College of the Adirondacks." We even talk about nature during breaks.

Conversation frequently centers on acid rain. The program and its location provide dramatic evidence of the seriousness of the issue. We learn there are no easy solutions to the problem, but we're all grateful for this opportunity to get the facts firsthand from experts. Milton ("the reverend") from Florida articulates our concern: "I've heard about acid rain for a long time, but now that I know what it's really all about I realize we've got to do something to deal with it."

All week the Elderhostelers talk about "the bog trip." The field trip will be a firsthand (or firstfoot) opportunity to see this increasingly rare and extremely important type of wetland. "It will be my only chance to walk on water," says Ray, a lawyer from Virginia.

In class, instructors Michael DeAngelo and Steve LaMere brief us on the details. There were probably as many as 215,000,000 acres of wetlands in the contiguous United States when European settlers arrived they tell us. Only 99,000,000 were left by the mid-1970s, when wetlands protection laws were enacted, and now less than that amount remains. DeAngelo and LaMere stress the many important roles wetlands play: as habitats for diverse animals and fish, as pollution filters, aids for flood control, and in supplying aquifers for drinking water. As our own field trip will prove, they are also valuable areas for educational, recreational, and aesthetic purposes.

Finally the day arrives, and we board a college van for the short drive. On the way we review the differences between marshes, bogs, peat bogs, and swamps (for example, the Everglades is a marsh, not a swamp). Our instructors assure us that what we are about to see is a true bog.

At the site we climb down a roadside embankment through thick, wet underbrush. Threading our way through the bushes, we make a snake of colorful headgear, rainwear, and boots. At the bog the brave ones wade through water and take tentative steps onto the bog mat. The wet ground undulates in response to each step, scattering birds in all directions. Just as Ray announces proudly that he's finally walking on water, Trisha from Virginia steps through the mat clear up to her waist. An Elderhostel rescue team is quickly at her side. When she is helped back to dry land, Trisha says with a smile, "Now I know what happened to Jimmy Hoffa."

## MONA ON SCOTLAND

"Jute, jam, and journalism made Dundee what it is," remarks instructor Mona Clark. She is a native of the city, on the east coast of

Scotland, and she ticks off its traditional industries with obvious pride. Her patriotism is even more evident when she speaks of "our country," emphasizing that this refers to Scotland alone, not England: "In the early days more Scottish people could read, write, and count than in England, where rhetoric was stressed. At the time of the American Revolution one-third of the population of Pennsylvania were Scots; nine of Washington's twenty-two generals were Scots. The impact on the world has been great for a very small country."

If Mona is at all representative of the forwardness and confidence of Scots in general, it is no surprise that their impact has been great. From the moment we arrive at the University of Dundee, Mona does everything possible to make us feel at home. The University is near the center of town, within easy walking distance of stores, pubs, and public buildings. We are housed in an old, but well-maintained brick residence hall directly across the street from dining and lounge facilities. Classes will be conducted a block away in a more modern academic building.

After our first dinner together, we are officially welcomed by university representatives and provided an orientation for the days ahead. We are briefed on the history of the university, the physical setting, and plans for class and field trips. We are told that our biggest danger will not come from wandering the streets—which are safe at any time of day or night—but rather from the unpredictable Scottish weather.

When the orientation session is over, we have a chance to introduce ourselves and hear about our previous experiences in Elderhostel programs. All sixteen of us, it turns out, are Americans. As might be expected in an international program, most of us have traveled abroad on a number of occasions. We spend the evening trading stories about unexpected travel experiences, unintended overtipping in foreign currency, unsolicited friendly assistance with a confusing map, and sharing advice about great art galleries and bargain restaurants.

Herb and Ruth are from New Jersey. They report that they have been to thirty-five programs and have also introduced thirty-eight couples to Elderhostel. "All but one couple loved it and that one couple said that they just had an OK experience."

Helen and David from Phoenix explain their process for attending Elderhostel programs: "We do a lot of reading ahead of time and focus on the possibilities, then choose a program and go to it, then go home and read and reflect, and then start looking around for another one."

This is a group of thoughtful and experienced travelers, hardly the types who would make a comment like the one overheard by our group leader, Ian Cox: "What a pity that they built the castle so close to the railway."

In the Elderhostel catalog our course was entitled "Scotland: Story of a Nation," but it might just as well have been listed simply as, "Mona on Scotland." In our morning classes Mona displays an impressive knowledge of Scottish history, economics, political science, and popular culture, but it is her enthusiasm and unabashed Scottish chauvinism that are truly the heart of our course. As she rolls along, inserting side comments as frequently as main points, Mona stops, rather embarrassed, and says with a modest smile, "But then, I'm just 'blethering,' you know."

We begin with a brief introduction to the Gaelic language. Mona pronounces the strange but melodious words, insisting that we learn the phrases for "How are you?", "Very well," "Thank you," and "Cheers!" She grins as she says the last word ("Slainthe," but pronounced "slansha"), admitting that it will probably cover the need for the first three in most cases. After all, this is a country where the word for whiskey means "water of life."

Next, we get an overview of early Scottish history: from the settlement of the west coast in about 8000 B.C. through raids, wars, and alliances, the establishment of Scottish Universities (Saint Andrews in 1412, Glasgow in 1451, Aberdeen in 1495, and Edinburgh in 1582) and the Union of the Parliaments in 1707, all the way to modern times. We are introduced to the class system, the origins of Scottish Protestantism, the economy of the earlier years, and the continuing difficulty of "making a go of it in this beautiful but rather inhospitable land."

At one point a confused hosteler raises his hand and says, "I'm having trouble taking notes on this last section you covered. Have I lost the thread or are you just blethering again?" Mona laughs and responds, "The answer to both questions is probably 'yes.'"

Special events during the week are an evening lecture by Professor William Marshall on Robert Burns and other Scottish literary figures; *Educating Rita*, a humorous film about a lower class Scotswoman's effort to improve her life by matriculation at the Open University; an evening at the theater; a tour of Dundee; excursions to Glasgow, Edinburgh, and Saint Andrews; and the requisite visit to the ancient Glenturret Distillery.

Near the end of the week, Mona hands out a sheet listing thirty-two "Great Scots," apparently to back up her frequent claims that "We were the first to do that," or "That was invented by a Scot, you know." The impressive list includes: Alexander Graham Bell; John Paul Jones; David Hume; Adam Smith; James Watt; John Macadam of road surfacing fame; Alexander Fleming, who discovered penicillin; and, admittedly unknown to anyone in the class, James Chalmers, who developed the adhesive postage stamp. Mona tempers her pride in this list by noting the continuing loss of Scottish population to immigration and the "brain drain." She admits, "Scotland is a hard place to live."

My wife and I are scheduled to appear at another program at the University of Durham and thus have to leave Dundee before the conclusion of the week. We board an early train and cross the long bridge over the Firth of Tay, morning cups of coffee in our hands. Wistfully we watch the town recede across the expanse of water, feeling like we've known Dundee for far more than a week. As a farewell tribute we lift our cups to the window with a hearty "Slansha, Dundee . . . Slansha, Mona!"

# CHAPTER TWO

# THE VISION

It was a hot, dry afternoon in eastern Australia. The ribbon of road stretched away across the endless and desolate countryside. Standing at the side of the road, backpack at his feet, was a man with long, thick white hair and a full white beard—somewhere between Santa Claus and an elderly hippie. He had been there most of the afternoon, waiting for the infrequent cars to pass and trying unsuccessfully to hitch a ride.

Finally, a car stopped. The driver was a severe-looking older woman who stared straight ahead, her hands tight on the wheel. The hitchhiker tossed his backpack in and gratefully accepted the ride. Before driving forward, the woman spoke, still looking straight ahead: "You know, I've never done this before, but I thought you looked so old you wouldn't be a danger to anyone."

The elderly hippie was Martin P. Knowlton, cofounder and first director of Elderhostel. Marty delights in telling this story, playing up the irony of the woman's remark. Although certainly not the type to cause ride-givers alarm, Marty most definitely considers himself "dangerous"—and growing more so with each year. In his restless, creative, and socially intrusive view of life, Marty has always challenged himself and others to fulfill the promise of life at all ages. It is perfectly understandable that in his later years Marty should be hitchhiking in Australia. It was with exactly this spirit of adventure and defiance of convention that he and his colleague David Bianco created Elderhostel.

Looking back, Marty's life could be read as one long process of preparation for his crucial role in founding Elderhostel; the list of travels and educational experiences on his resume rivals that of any Elderhostel catalog. Marty was born in 1920 in Dallas, Texas. While in college, he enlisted in the Free French Forces and served in the Middle East from 1940 to 1942, receiving the Croix de Guerre in Syria in 1941. For the next three years he served with the U.S. Army, receiving the Silver Star in the Philippines in 1944.

After his stints in the military, Marty returned to school and earned his B.A. in history and English literature at Birmingham Southern College. He subsequently was awarded an M.A. in political science and economics from the University of North Carolina at Chapel Hill, and did extensive graduate work in anthropology at Yale University and in education at Boston University. At various times before founding Elderhostel Marty taught government at the University of North Carolina, served as assistant director of Human Relations Area Files at Yale, conducted engineering research for the paper industry in Maine, and taught and coached at various secondary schools—at one point guiding the Brookline (Massachusetts) High School chess team to a national championship. Finally, he served as chief advisor to resident students at Boston University, where he began his long association with David Bianco.

David, who had graduated from Eastern Michigan University in 1966, was a graduate student in education at BU during the late 1960s and director of the university's residence hall system. Marty and David became acquainted through their work with the residential student programs and soon became close friends. "We were both rather unconventional in our thinking," David explained, "and I guess you could say we were good for each other, even though we had lots of differences." As was true of many undergraduate students during that time, they were both impatient with the status quo and used each other as sounding boards to explore "ways to make education more significant."

They had strenuous give-and-take debates that resulted in a co-authored article, which Marty and David published in the *Journal of*

Elderhostel cofounder Marty Knowlton. (Photo courtesy of Elderhostel)

*Education* in 1969. In this article the roots of the thinking that led to the birth of Elderhostel are quite visible. Entitled "A Proposal: An Institute of International Life at Boston University," the essay was a call to the American educational establishment to be more responsive and more responsible to the students it served. Marty and David made no attempt to hide their feelings about institutionalized higher education, beginning the article with the blunt statement: "No great sense of history is needed to perceive that the traditional university died twenty-five years ago. . . . When the balance sheet of unmet needs and unanswered challenges is finally totalled, the bankruptcy of the education establishment will be unmistakably clear." [1]

However, the article was by no means a self-indulgent tirade against the powers-that-be; it was a carefully planned, constructive proposal. Marty and David outlined a plan for the creation of an Institute of International Life at BU to foster international education, coordinate "area studies" departments, facilitate study abroad, and provide services for foreign students and faculty.

Even at such an early point, Marty and David had a vision that travel and education could be integrated into a more meaningful learning experience. Significantly, they placed their international institute within the School of Education. Addressing the value of undergraduate junior years abroad they wrote: "On a small scale, the value of this kind of experience/education combination has been demonstrated time and again by the returning veteran, the temporary dropout, and various work-study programs." (And, one might add now, the Elderhosteler.)

David has commented on the relationship between this early work and his subsequent collaboration with Marty in founding Elderhostel: "More than simply revising the entire field of international education we had struck upon an approach using what already existed and tried to make it better. This notion of not reinventing the world was to be the keystone to our vision of an Elderhostel." Perhaps Marty and David's vision is best stated in a summary paragraph of their premiere article that refers specifically to their proposed International Institute, but could just as easily apply to Elderhostel:

The Institute of International Life must have the freedom to be swiftly adaptable to students' needs, to be boldly initiatory of new forms and programs and sequences of education, to be inventive and experimental in administration, to be flexible and sensitive in responding to a changing world, and to be able to look on its mistakes as opportunities for learning rather than threatening disasters.[2]

After this collaboration, Marty and David went their separate ways for a few years. Marty began a four-year backpacking trip in Europe, where he participated in archaeological digs at nineteen sites in England and West Germany. David served for three years as dean of freshmen at Brandeis University and then, in 1972, began his seven-year stint as director of residential life at the University of New Hampshire.

In 1974, as president of the University of New Hampshire, I called for a major effort to create programs that would utilize institutional resources during the summer. In the context of this campus concern there were a number of promising initiatives, but none that could rival Elderhostel as developed by Marty Knowlton and David Bianco.

In July of that year, partly in response to meeting this addressed need, UNH hosted its second American Youth Hostel on campus. The program had been initiated by the residential life office at the university, and David had chosen his old friend, Marty, to be director. Together again, Marty and David revived their old philosophical debates, pushing each other to develop new initiatives for the improvement of education.

After giving eighteen-year-olds his best shot at Brandeis, Boston University, and UNH, David was somewhat burned out. Looking back, he explains: "I have to admit to some cynicism. We spent enormous money on educating the young; they take the system (at least they did in the 1960s) and compromise it; and they were always 18! I thought there had to be another way of educating that applies to other and eager learners." For his part, Marty was fresh back from Europe where he had become very well acquainted with the youth hostel programs and folk schools of Scandinavia. He was "impressed by the way in which

Cofounders Marty Knowlton and David Bianco during a recent visit to Elderhostel headquarters in Boston.

the availability of a network of modest accommodations encouraged and nurtured an adventuresome hosteling spirit in European youth. He also observed the very positive impact a *residential* setting had on adult education programs offered by the folk high schools."[3]

With all this as background, perhaps it is best to let Marty Knowlton describe what is certainly the critical moment in the establishment and naming of Elderhostel.

I was talking with . . . David, and I was telling him some of the experiences I'd had in Europe with older people, some of which David found rather exciting. And in a burst of enthusiasm, he said to me: 'This campus ought not to be having a youth hostel, it ought to be having an elder hostel!' And there was the day. It was one of those occasions, a serendipitous occasion. The name came first, and we put the program under it.

In order to appreciate the atmosphere in which these ideas came to life, it is necessary to have a picture of Marty and David's off-the-wall, but usually productive, working relationship. Though both men share a sincere concern about others and are idealistic in their outlook on life, they are markedly different in their character and working styles. Marty is socially and politically liberal, unpredictable, informal in attire, and quick to enter into discussions of ideas. David is slightly more cautious and is inclined to consider realistically the implications of his ideas. He is more administrative and organizational in his approach to issues.

Somewhat later, marriages having ended for each, Marty and David found it convenient to share a residence for several years. A stranger juxtaposition of personalities would be hard to imagine. David relates the "nerve wracking . . . way Marty would check book after book out of the library and completely forget about when they were due. His room was filled with books—all of them overdue. Marty was always checking them out faster than I could return them!"

David has joked that these two educational visionaries were truly "the original odd couple."

# CHAPTER THREE

# THE FIRST SUMMER

Marty and David spent many hours discussing the concept of Elderhostel, trying to determine what this nontraditional program should be and what it should not be allowed to become. They debated everything from the guiding philosophy to details of program content and cost. From the start, they agreed that it would be consistent with the European tradition of hosteling, based on the idea of residential programs with simple, affordable accommodations. With the belief that "when you're older you learn every bit as well as you ever learned . . . and probably better," the programs would have a strong and serious academic component, but courses would carry no credit.[1] Most important, Marty and David planned Elderhostel exclusively for older adults, setting an arbitrary minimum age requirement of sixty.

As the summer progressed, the brainstorming sessions grew to include an increasingly wider circle at the university. Marty and David consulted informally with various academic departments and with Vice-Provost for Academic Affairs David W. Ellis. Then Ellis, along with Vice-Provost for Student Affairs Richard Stevens and Director of Continuing Education Edward Durnall, came to me as president with the idea. We discussed what such a program might mean for the university and decided it was well worth pursuing.

At the beginning of August David sent letters to various people who were likely to be interested in the idea of hostels for the elderly. The letter—the first semipublic description of the concept—is quite interesting in light of the subsequent development of Elderhostel, both for its similarities to and its differences from the program that exists today.

Many of the basics were already there: elders would go to college campuses to attend week-long educational programs for the joint purposes of "self-enhancement" and the "development of an elderly cadre for 'community integration.'" However, the educational aspect of the program was not necessarily the main thrust. David's original proposal centered on the *hostel* concept, envisioning a network of self-service lodging facilities where elders would bring their own linens, do their own cooking and cleaning, and pay a very low fee in return. Elders could coordinate their stays at the hostels with the educational programs if they so desired, but they would not have to.

On August 9, 1974, those people who had responded favorably to David's letter were convened to discuss the concept. In addition to Marty and David and their assistant Karen Nixon, in attendance were representatives of University Extension Services, the New England Center for Continuing Education, the Resources Development Center and The New England Gerontology Center. The formal issue before the group was a "proposal to establish an American Elders Hostel Association and a program of Elder Hosteling."

The agenda of this early meeting ranged from a philosophical discussion of continuing education, to details of dorm use and meal facilities, to possible sources of funding. The group debated whether the hostel program should be billed as a New Hampshire program or a New England program.

It was decided that letters should be sent to residential life directors at all New England schools, as well as to a sample of elderly people, to determine what kind of program would be of most interest to them. Perhaps most significant at this first meeting was the proposal of "hostelships"—scholarships to be made available to elders who were interested in the program, but could not afford the fee. On the logistical end, the participants agreed that proposals for funding should be submitted to the Spaulding Potter Charitable Fund as well as to Title I, The Higher Education Act of 1965 (New Hampshire).

The resulting document, entitled "Elderhostel '75: A Proposal for Organizing and Operating a New Hampshire Network of Educational Hostels for the Elderly," was the first coherent statement of the goals and methods of Elderhostel. Signed by David Bianco and Charles Jellison, a UNH history professor who would teach one of the first courses, the proposal shows how remarkably well-developed the initial idea had become over the course of just a few months.

In a brief introductory section under the subhead "The Problem," the proposal documents the aging of the American population and resulting societal dilemmas. The authors concluded that "while it may be argued as to the degree to which the elderly have become a burden to society, it is patently clear that society has become a heavy burden to the elderly. This sense of burden, and the accompanying sense of alienation, will continue to grow unless new means of communication, avenues of re-entry and modes of participation are found."

The new modes of participation they had in mind, of course, were the proposed Elderhostel programs. The planned configuration for these programs was as follows: between mid-June and mid-August three one-week minicourses would be offered at each of five participating colleges (UNH-Durham, Franklin Pierce College, Keene State College, New England College, and Franconia College). The three courses would be an oral history seminar, an early American history course focusing on the local area, and a third elective course, to be determined by each school.

The oral history requirement was justified on the grounds that even among those elders most alienated from society, "there remains the rueful knowledge that they do have something of value that is uniquely of themselves to offer society—if they could only get someone's attention." * The early American history courses were designed to capitalize on the upcoming bicentennial celebrations, as well as to make the programs intensely local. Offerings for the third course ranged from

---

*The assumption that *all* elders are interested in recording their memories for posterity is now considered by some, Elderhostel President Bill Berkeley among them, to be somewhat condescending and ageist. At the time, however, the course was intended to convey respect for elders, and in fact turned out to be a very popular part of the program.

"The Psychology of Aging" and "The Conservation of Elderpower" to "Avocation in the Arts: A Survey."

In the rest of its almost thirty pages, the original Elderhostel proposal included detailed budgets, lists of steering committees, logistical arrangements, chains of command, and plans for the future. Marty and David's whimsical idea had grown into a full-fledged institutional endeavor.

Looking back, it is remarkable the degree to which the guiding philosophy expressed in this first proposal matches the spirit in which Elderhostel continues to operate. Sections of the proposal articulate Elderhostel's *raison d'etre* as well, if not better, than any subsequent attempts. These portions deserve to be quoted here at length:

> The sponsors of this program do not believe that retirement means withdrawal. Indeed, retirement should be viewed as an opportunity to enter new areas of life. Hostels have historically been places of temporary shelter and repose for people who are on the move. Elderhostel is for older people who are on the move, not necessarily or exclusively in terms of physical movement and travel, but in the sense of reaching out to new experience.*
>
> . . . On-campus life is essential to the Elderhostel concept and its purpose. Elderhostel is not just another educational or recreational program, not just another piece of busy business for the idle elderly; it is a program of many interrelated elements that is consciously designed to stimulate in the elderly the idea that they are not *pinned* into the framework where society seems to thrust them, but can step out and become part of, even creators of, new frameworks. It is the Elderhostel view that destruction of the idea that old age is static is a pressing obligation of the educational community.

A proposal so engaging was difficult to ignore. The Spaulding Potter Charitable Fund responded with a grant of $7,500. In addition, $22,000 in federal funds were made available through the Title I program, allowing hostelers sixty-five years and older and those on social security to attend the programs without paying tuition. Both Marty and David give credit to the late Professor William Henry who, as director of the Resources Development Center, was helpful in gain-

---

*This sentence is so fitting that it is still used, almost word-for-word, in the Elderhostel catalogs.

ing this support.* Former University of New Hampshire president, the late Arthur Adams, was another whose efforts to secure funding were keenly appreciated.

After months of uncertainty, the means were finally available by which it was possible to launch Elderhostel '75. When the grants came through, however, the preparations were by no means complete. There was much work still to be done, as David remembers:

Marty and I hit the road. Marty took off in the direction of the five campuses we had been in touch with for weeks, to share the good news and to shore up the preliminary arrangements. He made countless trips not only to the colleges involved but throughout New England, visiting community centers, libraries, and meal sites to promote the upcoming summer. I wrote articles for the Association of College and University Housing Officers and addressed the regional conference in February of 1975.

Between the trips, and the continual communications between the interested parties, Marty and I had to continue to define and develop the rationale, objectives, purposes, philosophy, and organizational minutiae of Elderhostel.

While David and Marty were out soliciting support, staff members Gayle Kloosterman and Karen Nixon held the fort at home, distributing 20,000 brochures and leaflets, contacting the media, and sending letters to countless potential supporters. Marty recalls that Gayle "did a tremendous job of managing things and deserves great credit, because I simply wasn't cut out to be an administrator."

Perhaps Gayle's most interesting task was sending letters to celebrities who, it was hoped, might serve as Elderhostel spokespersons. To Lawrence Welk she wrote, "Because of your personal popularity with the elderly, your approval of Elderhostel '75 could help significantly in our recruitment drive." To Lillian Hellman Gayle began, "Because I am a great admirer of your nonstop approach to living, I am sending you the enclosed information about Elderhostel '75." Gayle sent similar letters to Dick Cavett, Carol Burnett, former United States Senator George

---

*It was William Henry who suggested that the name of the program be routinely capitalized in order to give it a special, bold appearance. This convention is still followed in all Elderhostel literature.

Aiken, John Updike, and May Sarton (whose positive response initiated a long association with Elderhostel, including Sarton's eventual service on the Board of Directors).

The Elderhostel planners were also successful in selling their story to the media. The program was discussed on the "Good Morning" television show in Boston, leading to numerous inquiries from residents of that city. In April the Associated Press wires carried a story about the birth of Elderhostel, which appeared in the *Portsmouth Herald* and other papers.[2] In the article Elderhostel was described as a program "aimed at erasing the idea the elderly are 'all used up.'" Interestingly, Marty Knowlton was quoted as saying that he didn't expect many elders to take all three courses in the program. This sentiment was also reflected in a promotional question-and-answer flyer, in which the response to "Do you *have* to attend classes?" is: "No. You do your own thing, plan your own time. You may sign up for one or more . . . of the one-week courses . . . or you may wander about the campus in a completely unscheduled way doing whatever you want." *

After all the paperwork and letters, the interviews and the rush to spread the word, the Elderhostel crew was exhausted. Very low initial enrollments did nothing to improve their spirits. But as the first eager hostelers began to arrive, a remarkable transformation occurred. Marty Knowlton recalls:

We worked like slaves trying to generate an audience for our courses. And the first Elderhostel met and there were only six people. But we held it—we lasted through the week. We were delighted with the experience and so were the hostelers.

And the next week, there were seven. And the next week, because the first week group had gone home and begun to talk about it, we had thirteen in the class. And after the fourth week of Elderhostel, for the rest of the summer season we were filled right up and were beginning to turn people away.

---

*At the time, the "school" aspect of the program was being deemphasized in an attempt to attract a broader, less educated clientele. In later years, as it became increasingly clear that Elderhostelers were somewhat self-selecting, this orientation was revised, and participation in classes is now expected.

By the end, 220 hostelers had attended that summer (over 300, including commuters). They were pioneers, with all of the verve and spirit the term implies. Their positive attitude was more than enough to carry everyone through the requisite first-run administrative glitches.

After months of trying to anticipate what elders would respond to, it was immensely rewarding to Marty, David, and the others to hear what hostelers thought of the actual experience. By and large their reactions were in line with what the planners had hoped.

• "I came because I'm interested, because I like to learn all I can" said Gladys Larson, a 67-year-old kindergarten teacher.[3]

• Contrasting Elderhostel with typical summer resorts for the elderly, retired manufacturer Nathan Baker said, "I wasn't sitting in a rocking chair waiting to go in to eat again." Baker also commented on one of the aspects of the program that hostelers found most worthwhile, the chance to be with other elders. "There is nothing better than getting together with a group of your contemporaries and being able to talk to them like one of the family."[4]

• One hosteler, asked by a newspaper interviewer if she would recommend Elderhostel, said, "That's the whole trouble. I'm afraid they'll be so many who will hear about it that it may be difficult to get in next year."

This woman could not have known how true her hunch would prove to be. In fact, Elderhostel '75 was such a success that the inquiries for the next summer's program began coming in almost immediately after the hostels closed. These inquiries were spurred largely by word-of-mouth advertising in the vast elder network, as well as by media coverage, including an article in the *New York Times*.[5] Eventually more than sixty newspapers printed articles about Elderhostel '75.

In the mad rush to cope with inquiries and logistics for the next year's program, Marty and David struggled to step back and evaluate the program that had just been completed. With Gayle's help they put together a preliminary report on Elderhostel '75 in order to assess its successes and failures.

Making a point in class at Franklin Pierce College in New Hampshire.

Perhaps most telling was the fact that, when asked if he or she planned to return to Elderhostel in 1976, every single participant said "yes." Thus was begun a pattern of multiple program attendance that might well be termed "Elderhostelism." As one hosteler put it, "We're all recidivists. As soon as they let us out we find a way to get back in again."

Furthermore, in direct refutation of the "used-up elderly" myth, the hostelers showed great vigor and enthusiasm for the educational aspect of the program. "The only dissatisfaction was with courses of low intellectual content, and there were only one or two of these . . . The simpleminded, elementary approach was viewed, rightly, as condescending and rejected out of hand." Other bugaboos were laid to rest by the first summer's program:

Elderhosteler health was excellent; there were no illnesses, and only three accidents that were referred to a doctor for examination. Elderhostelers ate college food and delighted in it. Elderhostelers found present-day, college-variety "hippies" to be nonthreatening and largely nonoffensive . . . even rather nice.

There were very few aspects of Elderhostel '75 which could be viewed as failures. There were no hostelers from Vermont, but this was easily explained by poor promotion in that state. It was observed that when groups increased to twenty or more hostelers, divisive subgrouping occurred; the next year groups would be kept small to eliminate this problem.

The single most disturbing fact for Elderhostel planners, although by no means a surprise, was the overwhelmingly high economic status of participants. As the preliminary report stated, "The fact that relatively few Elderhostelers were from the lower economic groups . . . did represent a failure for the program. This is a problem with which Elderhostel '76 will have to cope in a much more realistic fashion." Marty Knowlton commented further on this issue to a journalist in the fall of 1975.

We are planning to obtain funding for scholarships for those who might not otherwise be able to attend. It is the consensus that those among the elderly who have most need of intellectual stimulation, who have the most urgent requirement for new pathways of reentry to society, who are most desperately trapped in the cul-de-sacs of nowhere—these are the ones who must be convinced that Elderhostel is for them.[6]

With a healthy awareness of these shortcomings, all those involved in the birth of Elderhostel agreed nonetheless that it had been a resounding success. In the course of that first summer's programs, Marty, David and the others had learned a great deal: they knew that courses and instructors had to be intellectually rigorous, that hostelers could enjoy the program regardless of their educational background, and that elders didn't mind spartanlike hostel accommodations. And as Marty has said, they learned "the real importance of Elderhostel: that it discovered Elderhostelers—no one knew they were there!"

# CHAPTER FOUR

# UNSOLICITED

# GENEROSITY

With one real experience behind them, the Elderhostel organizers were ready to plan for the future. The first summer's program had made their pipe dream a reality, proving by its overwhelming popularity that the idea at the core of Elderhostel was both meaningful and viable. Elderhostel '75 also served as a dry run, providing an example to study for benefits and drawbacks. The first programs received high praise from all corners, but there was also universal acknowledgment that improvements could be made.

The Elderhostel planners now knew what it felt like to run a program, and they all had their personal opinions about how smoothly things had proceeded. To augment these individual observations, they commissioned Betty Holroyd Roberts, a social scientist with no previous connection to the program, to conduct a more objective evaluation. The resulting paper, "A Report Evaluating the Effectiveness of Elderhostel '75," served as a starting point for the refined development of the organization.

Based on questionnaires, solicited and unsolicited letters, newspaper accounts, and interviews, Roberts evaluated Elderhostel's success in meeting its stated goals, such as providing low-cost, comfortable campus living for elders, and developing a curriculum geared especially for them. Roberts concluded "all stated goals were achieved that were financially viable," and went on to describe Elderhostel's successful achievement of a further, unstated goal: "having an impact on the community." As evidence for this final point, Roberts revealed some remarkable data, including:

1. Fifteen hundred requests for information and applications by February, 1976.

2. Two hundred forty inquiries from institutions such as the Library of Congress, Catholic Charities, Offices of Aging in nearly every state, community action agencies, senior citizen centers, and the Mayor's office of New York City.

3. The intent to participate in Elderhostel '76 by twenty-three new college campuses. In addition to these were requests to participate by 350 other colleges and thirty requests from community colleges. There were twenty more unspecified college contacts.[1]

Roberts's overall conclusions about Elderhostel '75 reflect the unique characteristic that continues to mark the organization today—the extraordinary congruence between the people and the program. Finding it impossible to condense the phenomenon of Elderhostel into objective, sociological lingo, Roberts instead relied upon the words of Elderhostelers themselves. Commenting simply that "something happened which was very positive," she took excerpts from the more than 100 letters hostelers had sent in to that date:

- I had a very *happy* time at Elderhostel.
- . . . Two happiest weeks in many, many years.
- . . . It filled the void of loneliness I had been living in.
- For the past two years I have been most uncomfortable and somehow that week took care of so many of my problems. My balance improved to an amazing degree; pains of two years' duration vanished in the excessive heat. I returned with more energy than I have had in two years—and looking better than I have since 1965.

Perhaps more telling than the reactions to the summer of '75 program was the hostelers' commitment to the continuation of Elderhostel. In various ways, those who returned the questionnaires said:

- May the concept flourish in the entire U.S.!
- Call on us if we can foster your program in this area.
- I will speak to Senior Citizens groups about it.

Between the end of the first program in August 1975 and early spring of 1976, over 1,000 letters had been sent to Elderhostel by the 300 "alumni." The letters were as astonishing in content as they were in number. The staff observed at the time that, "Repeatedly they tell . . . of new involvement with community action groups, volunteer organizations, and educational opportunities. Several mention 'first time ever' involvement in politics . . . Always there is mention that Elderhostel is responsible for these new activities."[2]

These letters were gratifying to Marty, David, and all of us who were involved with Elderhostel. Clearly, Elderhostel was doing what it set out to do and more. Just as we had anticipated, there was a vast constituency of elders looking for broader opportunities than those offered by the mainstream, ageist society.

In fact, the success of the first summer was somewhat troubling to Marty and David—it made them realize the incredible power the program could wield. "It was, in truth, a bit too successful to be entirely reassuring," they wrote in a planning document, "so we were not without apprehension as we set out to answer [a] new set of questions as to whether Elderhostel could be replicated on a broader scale."

Apprehensive or not, the Elderhostel crew discussed the possibilities and came up with a tentative set of plans for 1976 and beyond. With the protective caveats that expansion be limited initially to the six New England states, supervised by the Board of Directors, and monitored by objective evaluations, they outlined the following program goals.

1. To develop capacity for 3,000 to 4,000 participants in New England without reducing the quality of the program.

2. To expand in 1977 into a national organization, coordinating numerous regional networks.

3. To increase participation from lower economic and lower activity-level groups, by means of increased hostelships ($17,000 in 1976).

4. To make Elderhostel independent of outside funding by 1978.

These goals assumed almost exponential growth in the programs, but this assumption was entirely in keeping with the reality of the public response. By this point—less than a year after the first summer program—unsolicited inquiries from institutions wishing to develop Elderhostel courses had been received from as far away as California, Michigan, Illinois, and Canada. Ricker College in Houlton, Maine had even proposed the idea of running Elderhostel courses in the winter. Everybody wanted in.

Furthermore, the Elderhostel planners had already begun to observe an almost magical commitment to the organization from all parties involved, which made even the most unlikely sounding propositions possible. From the beginning, Elderhostel had been the recipient of abundant generosity: first from UNH in its provision of an office, WATS line for long-distance phone service, borrowed cars, and meeting space, and then from the Spaulding Potter Charitable Fund in its grant of $7,500. Everybody involved with the project seemed willing to give and give without asking anything in return.

Throughout the first year, Elderhostel operated with only 1 paid employee, and that one, the Director, on less than ½ pay . . . Every member of the Board of Directors felt badly over-committed at the time they were asked to join the Board, yet no one who was asked refused . . . some travelled hundreds of miles [for the first meeting] without reimbursement.

Although no campaign has begun for hostelships yet, $3,150 in pledges is in hand . . . Several participating schools have offered to take without charge "a few" individuals who cannot pay—"unbooked hostelships" we call these.

. . . Ricker College . . . has announced itself ready to absorb the cost of the courses for two weeks of Elderhostel, if necessary. And, Franconia College, forever on the verge of bankruptcy, has offered to hold an extra week of Elderhostel, without compensation for courses, if needed.

Repeatedly, unsolicited generosity has marked the history of Elderhostel. People and institutions like the program and seem to like the spirit which animates it. Much is said today about put-your-money-on-the-line, balance-sheet education, but such unstinting commitment and dedication to a program that

45

does not have a spare nickel in it for anyone says something very, very nice for the people and institutions in higher education in New England.[3]

In less than a year of full-time operation Elderhostel had taken on a life of its own. Although its creators could guide the direction in which the organization would move, it was clear that Elderhostel already belonged to far more people than just Marty or David; it belonged to every program director, administrator, teacher, and hosteler who had in any way been involved.

# CHAPTER FIVE

# INSTANT

# MOMENTUM

Although they had consciously laid the groundwork for rapid expansion, nothing could have prepared Marty, David, and the Elderhostel crew for the tidal waves of enthusiasm their venture put in motion. In 1975 the five New Hampshire colleges had offered fifteen weeks of programs for the 220 participants. In 1976 twenty-one colleges in six states offered sixty-nine program weeks to 2,000 enrollees and another 2,000 applicants were turned away. By the third summer, sixty-one colleges in twelve states offered 156 program weeks and there were almost 6,000 applicants for 4,800 enrollment openings.

Marty, of course, was the main reason for the growth problems. An educational Johnny Appleseed, he was off spreading the word about late-life potential to anyone who would listen. Colleges, universities, and continuing education associations responded to his charismatic appearance on behalf of Elderhostel. "That bearded fellow from New Hampshire," as one letter described him, was all over the map. Programs began to pop up in North Carolina, Iowa, and other states far beyond New England.

Soon, the staff—such as it was—found itself handling 200 to 450 inquiries a day. The mail was piling up, unanswered, and the phone was ringing constantly. It seemed as though every American over the age of sixty wanted to hear about Elderhostel. None of them could have realized that Elderhostel was really just four people, working mostly without pay, in borrowed office space.

Though Elderhostel already had the reputation of a sweeping edu-cational movement, the truth was that the fledgling organization was flying by the seat of its pants, barely making it through each day. Marty describes those early times as "exciting, surprising, and overwhelming." He recalls people "crowding in on us and wanting more than we were prepared to make available. It was a frantic time."

The "instant momentum," as Marty terms it, was exhilarating, but it obviously could not go on. With each new day it became more clear that the public demand for educational opportunities for elder citizens was far too vast to be handled by an organization without financial sup-port, home, charter, or paid staff. A writer reflected several years later, "it was obvious that people with the skill, talent, and taste for large scale administration had to take over the program's day-to-day man-agement, leaving the brainstormers to their more creative intellectual pursuits." [1]

Marty, for one, was particularly unhappy with the situation. Throughout his life he had always been incurably restless, a creative thinker with an inherent distrust of administration. When Elderhostel had been created according to his vision, he had never really considered the possibility that it would lead him to keep files, answer phones, and concentrate on organizational details. But the reality of the situation was that he *had* to. Gayle was doing all she could, but there was much more work than she alone could handle. David was busy with his re-sponsibilities as director of residential life for UNH and from that year (1977) on acted only as an unofficial advisor to Elderhostel.

When he began to realize how much administrative work was needed to keep Elderhostel going, Marty wanted out. The tensions were harm-ful to Marty's emotional state as well as to the young organization. He wrote at the time, "I'm trying to get out of Elderhostel . . . I know my inner feelings on administration are irrational. I tend to do damage by cutting administrative corners much too freely and by resisting, beyond all reason, needed administrative developments."

At this time Marty had a regular correspondence with William Berke-ley, then director of the Commission on Educational Issues, an initiative to encourage public and private secondary schools to cooperate rather than compete. Berkeley, a Yale graduate with an M.A. in education from Harvard, had long been involved in educational administration. Before assuming leadership of the Commission, he had for ten years directed A Better Chance, a national program designed to increase educational opportunities for underprivileged minority youth.

Berkeley's connection with Elderhostel had begun innocently enough in the fall of 1976 when a friend whose parents were planning to attend a program approached him at a conference. Knowing that Berkeley was involved in education, the friend asked him as a favor to check up on this crazy-sounding program to make sure it was legitimate. Berkeley obliged by tracking down Elderhostel's central address and writing the most basic of inquiry letters to Marty Knowlton. Marty responded with the standard brochures and other information, which Berkeley dutifully looked over for his friend. More than merely deeming Elderhostel "safe" for his friend's parents, Berkeley found the program immensely appealing. He wrote back to Marty, "I think yours is one of the most creative and worthwhile concepts I have run across in some time." He asked for more information, displaying from the start an interest in the administrative details and logistical problems of the organization.

An experienced educational administrator like Bill Berkeley was the perfect outlet for Marty's growing frustrations in running Elderhostel. A more vigorous correspondence ensued, and soon Bill went to UNH to visit the Elderhostel offices. He remembers:

I was really quite taken by Marty and Gayle. Their fervor and commitment seemed to be something right out of the sixties, and I guess, to some degree, I was missing the sort of visceral commitment which I had in my job when I was working at A Better Chance. Marty and Gayle served to remind me that there were good causes to defend and advocate beyond the institutional self interest of independent secondary schools. One thing led to another, and I found myself in more continual communication with Marty, trying to help him through a whole range of administrative problems that he was having, as well as to try to identify some sources of funding for him. I found it incredible that Marty was doing everything he was doing without receiving any pay, and I was anxious to see what I could do to help.

Bill assumed the role of "interested outsider," volunteering to share his experience in fund raising and other organizational necessities. He arranged a flurry of meetings with various grant sources, including the Ford Foundation, the Rockefeller Brothers Fund, the Lilly Endowment, the Sears Roebuck Foundation, and the Edna McConnell Clark Foundation—all in one month!

As helpful as it was, this kind of conventional organizing was completely alien to the rebellious, anti-establishment Marty. The clash of his free-lance, shoot-from-the-hip style and Bill's conventional administration is particularly evident in the story of Marty's request for money from the Aetna Insurance Foundation. Bill recalls:

My experience suggested that if Marty were to get a good and responsive hearing he ought to ask for $5,000. Perhaps, if he got a wildly enthusiastic response from the people at Aetna, he might be so bold as to ask for $10,000. I relayed that wisdom to him. The next day Marty called me back to report on the meeting and he said he really thought it went quite well. The people were impressed by him and impressed by the idea. I congratulated Marty and asked him how much money he had asked for. He said that he asked for $40,000! I said, Oh, Marty, you really blew it. I'm sure you will scare them off with a request that large! Of course, about three weeks later Marty received a letter from the head of the Foundation notifying him of a grant of $40,000! So much for the wisdom of the experienced fund raiser.

The clash of styles did not always end so productively, however. Though their overall goals and level of commitment were the same, Marty and Bill found themselves increasingly at odds with each other over matters of procedure. Bill's position as an "interested outsider" was particularly difficult. He explained that in trying to assist ". . . Marty on matters administrative and financial, I was attempting something very tricky. Could I, within the constraints of a full-time job and my own approach to fund raising and management, be of any real help to Elderhostel? Reluctantly, I came to the conclusion that I could not." Bill pulled away from Elderhostel and discontinued his fund raising efforts on the organization's behalf.

But the appeal of the idea was so strong that within a month Bill was back, determined to find a more appropriate role for himself. The opportunity came during a visit with Marty to the Ford Foundation in New York. As usual, Marty captivated his audience and a large grant was virtually assured. As they left the building, Bill commented how gratifying it must be for Marty to see his brainchild taking off so successfully. To the contrary, Bill remembers that

[Marty confessed he was] miserable with Elderhostel's success. His job in running the program had evolved into too much of an administrative nightmare, and he acknowledged that he was not a good administrator and wanted no part of taking Elderhostel into its next level of success. It was then that Marty turned to me and asked whether I would be interested in "taking over" Elderhostel. We talked a little more and, obviously, I knew that Elderhostel didn't really exist as an organization; I knew that Marty hadn't been paid for months, and I knew that to think seriously of some more official involvement with Elderhostel would be sheer folly on my part. However, I also knew that Elderhostel was one of those great ideas, and I began to fantasize about how somehow I might be able to work more effectively on behalf of the program." [2]

Once again using his skill in creative administration, Bill came up with a workable arrangement: the Commission on Educational Issues would serve as a temporary administrative home for Elderhostel. As director of the Commission, Bill would head a transition team to assume leadership of Elderhostel from Marty Knowlton. In assembling his team, it was natural that Bill would turn to an old friend. Mike Zoob was a graduate of Trinity College (Hartford) and Harvard Law School, and had worked closely with Bill at A Better Chance. Mike's initial response to Bill's request was that someone would have to be "absolutely nuts to seriously consider a move to a nonexistent organization to take on a nonexistent job at a nonexistent salary." Nevertheless, Mike agreed to attend a program and became "hooked by the incredibly infectious and compelling Elderhostelers."

Bill also contacted another friend, Jerry Foster, director of the Phillips Andover Academy Summer Session and a colleague at the Commission. The idea was that these three professionals together would make up the national staff of a revamped Elderhostel organization. In proposing this arrangement, Bill admitted at the time "that it is somewhat presumptuous to present ourselves as a 'package.' Yet it is my reasonably objective judgment that we represent an interesting and appropriate combination of backgrounds, experiences, and talents to establish a strong national Elderhostel program."

On September 10, 1977, a group of advisors—some old faces and some new—met and incorporated itself officially as the national Board of Directors of Elderhostel. Present were: Charles E. Odell, Sr., chairman of the Pennsylvania Council on Aging; Howard Jones, Headmaster of Northfield Mount Hermon School; Merrell M. Clark of the Edna McConnell Clark Foundation; Frank Manning, an elder activist and president of the Massachusetts Association of Older Americans; Eleanor Slater, a state legislator from Rhode Island; and Ollie Randall, one of the founders of the National Council on Aging. Also on the Board, though not present, were Mildred McAfee Horton, former president of Wellesley College and Chair of the initial New England Board, and writer May Sarton.*

Among its first actions, the Board voted to accept the resignation of Marty Knowlton as executive director and immediately appointed him a member of the Board. Then, having been briefed by Bill on his "presumptuous" package deal, the Board voted to offer him the job as national executive director of Elderhostel with "full authority to staff the National Office as he sees fit within . . . budgetary limitations."

So it was, Bill explains, that Elderhostel secured the services of "three very different people, fairly senior in age and experience, all of whom could count themselves as political liberals and social progressives, fresh from particularly interesting experiences during the sixties, and looking for a new 'special' involvement."[3] Howard Jones likes to talk about the "nationwide search" that produced Bill as the first head of Elderhostel, but the truth Bill says,

is that I got the position by default as the only one willing to try and get something going. When I think back on it, the idea of a forty-five-year-old man with

---

*Odell provided important leadership as the founding chair of the *next* Board of Directors from 1980 to 1984. The author became chair in 1984 and in 1990 the chair was assumed by David W. Ellis, president and director of the Boston Museum of Science. For the composition of the board as of March 4, 1992, see the Appendix on p. 185.

Elderhostel president Bill Berkeley.

a wife, a six-year-old daughter, an infant daughter, along with a house and a mortgage—for me to consider taking on a job which didn't exist with an organization which had no legal status, for a salary which couldn't be paid—that's a little scary. I was either very naive or very smart, thinking that this new educational idea, the product of the imagination of a self-styled guerilla educator, could support the families of three senior administrators in their forties.

Those three senior administrators were bold enough to risk their careers, based entirely on what their instincts told them about the potential of Elderhostel. Bill wrote in the first annual report of the "new" Elderhostel, "We eagerly accepted the offer, sensing in Elderhostel that rare combination of an extraordinary administrative challenge, coupled with an opportunity to be of service to a segment of the population whose needs were only beginning to receive proper attention nationally."[4]

To the three committed leaders, Elderhostel seemed an attractive marriage of administration and idealism; in time, the marriage between these men and Elderhostel would prove even more attractive.

# CHAPTER SIX

# A CAUSE FOR
# CELEBRATION

On July 1, 1978, Bill, Mike, Jerry, and a secretary began the full-time leadership of a newly independent Elderhostel, located in borrowed offices in Newton, Massachusetts. With the ink hardly dry on its organizational bylaws, trademark, and IRS-approved nonprofit status, the newly independent Elderhostel was ready to blossom in new and different directions.

However, as the trio of administrators soon learned, new and different was not necessarily what the loyal Elderhostel constituencies either wanted or expected. Most people's image of Elderhostel to that point had been completely and simply, Marty Knowlton. In his charismatic way, Marty had stimulated interest in the program across the country and in doing so had become the identity of the organization. Beyond Marty's personality and their particular Elderhostel experience(s), most people had no other understanding of Elderhostel.

Bill and the others had learned almost immediately after their introduction to Elderhostel that it would not be easy to follow in Marty's footsteps. In the fall of 1977, just after the first meeting of the Elderhostel Board at which it had been agreed that the three new administrators would be hired to launch a national Elderhostel office, Marty had invited a number of the just-appointed state directors to Boston for a meeting. Nothing had been done to tell the state directors ahead of time of Marty's desire to leave Elderhostel, of the appointment of a Board of Directors, of the plans to form an independent organization, or of the involvement of the three new staff members.

The state directors arrived for the meeting and right away Marty announced his withdrawal from active involvement with Elderhostel. Then the three future staff members were introduced as his successors. Everybody in the room was shocked. Bill Berkeley remembers:

There was a lot of anger and resentment and anxiety because no one had been prepared for this. I think there was some feeling that somehow Marty was being eased out. There certainly was a strong feeling that could be summarized with the following question—What were these three unknown characters saying about running Elderhostel when the people in the room thought they *were* Elderhostel? There was a lot of tension between the members of the grass-roots Elderhostel movement such as it was in those days and the three new 'boys from Boston' (as we were immediately dubbed—and it sure didn't help that we were all male!). A good two or three years were spent trying to reduce this tension between the national office and the growing corps of state directors.

In order to overcome the suspicion that the Boston group would be centralizing all operations and, in effect, undercutting the role of the state directors, steps were taken to involve those directors in the evolving organization. Recognizing the need to reassure the directors, chair of the Board Charles Odell negotiated a power-sharing agreement. As a result of meetings that Odell chaired, a steering committee was formed consisting of six state directors elected by their peers from six geographical regions. This committee was to work with Elderhostel management in areas of policy development and implementation. Furthermore, it was agreed that three members of the steering committee would serve as ex-officio members of the Board of Directors with full voting privileges. It was a fair and skillful solution to the complex feelings surrounding the transition to a national organization.

With the immediate crisis resolved, the new Elderhostel leadership still had numerous questions to address. There was need for a satisfactory office and for mechanisms of communication. Furthermore, there were fundamental procedural and policy issues to be confronted: What should be the separate responsibilities of a central office, a state office, and each individual campus? Is there need to trademark additional items representing Elderhostel? What actions are necessary in order to assure quality control of programs being offered? The challenge of maintaining program momentum was compounded by the need to build a new organization. And there was strong preliminary evidence that a very different kind of organizational model was needed.

The leaders could not just sit down and get to work, even though responding to these questions was vital to Elderhostel. Before a new structure for the organization could be implemented—indeed if the organization was to function at all—they needed money. Bill recalls, "We were prepared to run a tight ship, lean and mean, but no amount of thriftiness and good management could solve our basic problem: we needed money and we needed it immediately." So Mike Zoob "hit the foundation road."

Mike had already been on the payroll for a few months, thanks to a $30,000 grant from the AHS Foundation, a small family foundation in Cleveland. Now he began to look for other sources of funding. Drawing upon his previous experience as a fund raiser, Mike sent a letter to every member of the National Businessmen's Committee, a group of corporate leaders who had supported A Better Chance. One of these letters went to Thornton Bradshaw, president of Atlantic Richfield (ARCO), who asked William Kieschnick, then executive vice-president (and subsequently president) of ARCO, to investigate Elderhostel.

On Thanksgiving Day, 1977, Bill, Mike, and Jerry arranged to meet with Kieschnick at the John Harvard statue in Harvard Yard. When it became clear how much they had to discuss they borrowed a nearby office, where they stayed for three hours. Incredibly enough, a month later Elderhostel was notified of a $75,000 grant by ARCO. The money, credibility, and prestige associated with this grant were extraordinarily important in launching the fledgling organization.*

Boosted by this first success, Mike and Bill continued to explore every reasonable lead. It was encouraging that foundation officials always seemed to be interested in the program, but competition was intense. Where Marty had relied solely on his personal charisma and

---

* William Kieschnick subsequently became a member of the Elderhostel Board of Directors and continued to make corporate support by ARCO possible. This personal and corporate support proved crucial to the early growth of the organization.

Elderhostel vice-president Mike Zoob.

entrepreneurial spirit, Mike and Bill played a more conventional game, working contacts and tapping the networks with which they were already familiar. In their proposals to potential donors, they made heavy use of the vast number of testimonials by Elderhostelers, letting the program speak for itself.

The new leaders were aided by Elderhostel's many well-connected friends. Board member Merrell M. Clark of the Edna McConnell Clark Foundation (and more recently president and chief executive officer of Elderworks in Scarsdale, New York) supported proposals to many foundations. Clark also brought to the Elderhostel Board Curtiss Frank, the former president of Dun and Bradstreet, and Willard L. Boyd, president of the University of Iowa, who in turn contacted their own fund raising connections. If there was money available anywhere, somebody in this growing Elderhostel network was bound to know about it.

A major breakthrough occurred on September 7, 1978 when word was received that the Kellogg Foundation had approved a $300,000 grant to Elderhostel. Bill Berkeley accepted the money gratefully, commenting that it was "absolutely essential to the successful development of Elderhostel into a truly national program of major significance. . . . With these resources, Elderhostel can be made available to literally tens of thousands of older adults who know that growing old does not mean that you have to stop growing."

The little Elderhostel organization had scored a big victory by gaining support from a prestigious national foundation. What had to this point been a day-to-day effort substantially run on good will, faith, and volunteer (or near-volunteer) labor was transformed overnight into a professional, national organization. A new office was established at 100 Boylston Street in downtown Boston, which would remain Elderhostel's home for six years.

With a new office and money in the bank (at least temporarily), all that remained for the three relatively experienced generalists who made up the Elderhostel staff was to learn what a national office was supposed to do. They were not even sure what skills would be needed to run such a venture. None of the men had training in continuing or older adult education, nor in issues surrounding the institutional environment of higher education. Mike Zoob said, "Our knowledge of these critical areas was something less than negligible."

Meanwhile, there were a few thousand elders who were writing, phoning, and visiting the little office in hopes of gaining admission to programs. If Elderhostel was to keep faith with its constituents, everything needed attention right away.

This was easier said than done because the office was by no means a smooth-running system. Berkeley and Zoob have characterized this initial period in the national office as "a Keystone Kops kind of operation. We had to learn a lot on the job and, of course, we sometimes fell all over each other." Anne Maida, who was hired early on as Bill Berkeley's "chief cook and bottle washer" (and who is still his executive assistant), remembers that walking into the new national office was like "coming into a motherless home . . . They didn't even have printed return envelopes!"

It wasn't merely a lack of supplies that was bogging down the office. The near-exponential growth in programs and participants had made Elderhostel's whole organizational system somewhat obsolete. At the time each state, through its state office, published its own catalog and provided registration services for hostelers interested in attending a program in that state. This had worked fine in 1975 for New Hampshire, in 1976 when the program encompassed all of New England, and even in 1977 when fourteen states offered programs. But by 1978 many hostelers were complaining that they had to write to several different states for catalogs and then register separately with each office. Just as it had initially made sense for a state office to coordinate information and registration materials on behalf of the individual institutions within that state, it now became evident that a national system was needed to incorporate the many statewide systems.

Coordinating the registration for every Elderhostel program in the country was no easy task. With enrollments already in the tens of thousands, every step in the process took on monumental proportions. To help with the manual labor, Northeastern University students were hired on their co-op terms. One of those students was Diann Bouthot, now registrar of Elderhostel. Diann recalls the giant board that was up at registration time, with pegs for each Elderhostel program, and tags on each peg representing the space for one participant. As each Elderhostel staffer leafed through the applications he or she would call out "Give me a Miami" or "I need two Williams," and would be handed the appropriate tags. The process would continue until all the pegs were empty of tags.

In retrospect the process seems quaint and perhaps even fun, but sorting registrations by hand was a laborious task, which took up valuable time that could have been better spent elsewhere. The enthusiastic and technologically innocent executives of Elderhostel could see the handwriting on the wall—it would be necessary to "go electronic."

At first they tried "sharing" time on other organizations' computers, a common practice before personal computers became readily available. But this proved almost more of a hassle than doing everything by hand. For example, in order to get a printout of the mailing list, Elderhostel staffers first had to send a list of new names to the nearby bank whose computer mainframe they used. A few days later, the bank would send back a computer tape with the information encoded on it. Then this tape was sent to a firm in New York that could print out an actual list. Finally, the printed labels were returned to the Elderhostel offices in Boston to be put on envelopes and mailed. This cumbersome system made it all the more obvious that Elderhostel needed a computer of its own.

The staff began interviewing vendors, finally selecting an advanced word processor manufactured by a major computer company. This was long before the days of miniaturization, and the hulking machine filled virtually one side of the office. In preparation for the arrival of the new equipment, the Elderhostel leadership had been told that the computer would need a "dedicated" line to plug into. It was only after some investigation that they discovered that the term referred to an electrical line running directly from the central source and that would not have to compete with other equipment or appliances for the "pure" current that the new equipment required. Such a dedicated line was installed with a bright red plate to distinguish it from its less committed, undedicated neighbor.

As the modernization of the office approached, excitement grew among the staff. Anne Maida remembers that the atmosphere in the office was like that in a "big family, about to get a new T.V." When the computer was installed, however, all the problems were not immediately solved. Bill Berkeley remembers:

The much anticipated day arrived. The machine which would turn our office into a reasonable replica of the Johnson Space Center was delivered and installed by a team of experts from the manufacturer. We were off and running. Almost immediately we knew all was not right with our new helper. Records typed in could be reproduced one minute and would disappear the next—and for no apparent reason. Participant rosters to be sent to each institution hosting an Elderhostel program changed inexplicably from hour to hour. We called the service number, the service representative came to our office promptly, and, after tinkering for a half an hour or so, he pronounced the machine fixed. He declined to say what he had found wrong. The malfunctioning continued. We thereupon embarked on a dizzying escalator ride up the ranks of service personnel from the manufacturer. Ever more impressive people with ever more impressive titles and credentials came to view the patient and try to repair the damage. Hour-long telephone consultations with the international service headquarters in a far-off state didn't seem to help.

All during this time the building maintenance man had been observing the comings and goings, the wringing of hands, the hundred telephone conversations, with a bemused look on his face. Finally, he ambled over to the head of the service team and pointed to the outlets on the wall. There was the newly installed but still virginal dedicated line with its bright red identifying plate and, next to it, the regular outlet with our fancy, high-tech equipment plugged in . . . sharing its "undedicated" electricity with our office coffee pot! The fancy service personnel who installed the equipment had plugged it into the wrong receptacle! The red-faced service man walked over, switched the plug to the dedicated line and our wonderful machine hummed appreciatively with no further malfunctions. What a magnificent introduction into the mysteries of modern office technology![1]

With an efficient, modern national office a reality, the Elderhostel leadership was finally able to concentrate on its real priority: affordable, innovative educational programs for elders. The goal which they set their sights on had been proposed by Merrell Clark at an early Board of Directors meeting: the establishment of an Elderhostel presence in every state of the union. This goal guided the overall planning of the organization, but the individual who took it upon himself to implement the logistics was Jerry Foster.

Jerry was on the road constantly in those days—attending continuing education meetings, making speeches, trying to solicit interest in Elderhostel—and living out of suitcases the entire time. As soon as one or more colleges from the same state expressed interest in hosting Elderhostel, Jerry would set up a meeting. He would fly out to a central location, make a presentation, and more than likely select a state director, all during the same trip.

In 1980 it began to look as if the once seemingly impossible goal would be achieved. Every single state was now a part of the Elderhostel network, except for New Jersey. Despite the number of colleges and universities there, not one serious inquiry had come from the Garden State. Finally, a rather casual letter of interest arrived and Jerry was off in a flash to investigate. No doubt the innocent inquirer from New Jersey was a bit startled by the speed and determination of Jerry's response—but not so startled he wasn't hooked on the program. The arrangements were made in record time and Elderhostel was at last truly a national network, with a presence in all fifty states.

In just five years, Elderhostel had grown from an interesting notion into a vast, highly visible, functioning educational movement. The significance of the achievement was perhaps best captured by gerontology writer Max Kaplan, writing in 1981 in *Change* magazine: "The momentum of Elderhostel, after half a decade, is irreversible. Its impact is ultimately immeasurable, as all humanistic advance is immeasurable. But it is real all the same, and a cause for celebration."[2]

# CHAPTER SEVEN

# THE 1980s:

# A DECADE OF

# EXPANSION

In the fall of 1981 the Board of Directors met in Boston and was informed that earlier reports of prospective enrollments had been too conservative. The surprising growth of Elderhostel was continuing, and campus coordinators, state directors, and the Boston staff had spent the summer months in a valiant effort to keep the organization together in the face of exploding demand. Chair Charles Odell looked at his Board colleagues around the table and said, "Who knows where this is going to end? Ladies and gentlemen, let me make it official—we have a winner on our hands."

There was no doubt that Elderhostel was a winner. The program design was right, the timing was right, and increasing thousands of elders knew it. They said so in the most direct manner possible—by registering. For every person who had participated in the first summer's program, there were now 150 elders enrolled in courses across the country.

Now firmly established as both a professional business and a nationwide educational movement, Elderhostel changed gears. With a steady growth rate, committed full-time staff, and a national reputation on which to rely, the organization began what most corporations would consider "normal" operations. In addition to the continued growth and success of the original programs, the 1980s saw new initiatives which have greatly affected the development of Elderhostel. The three most significant of these initiatives were the move to *financial independence*, the creation of *international programs*, and the establishment of *Elderhostel Canada*.

## FINANCIAL INDEPENDENCE

The excitement of growth during the early years was always tempered by the depressing realization that the organization would fail if corporate and foundation support disappeared. Bill Berkeley and Mike Zoob put an enormous amount of time and energy into the search for funds and were remarkably successful in gaining support. From 1977 to 1984 Elderhostel received a total of $2,090,000 from twenty-six corporations and foundations—an impressive endorsement.

But hustling for grants was a tiring, uncertain proposition. Bill and Mike felt they spent too much time asking for money and not enough time planning educational travel programs for elders. So in spite of their notable success in winning grant moneys, they sought a means by which Elderhostel would gradually wean itself from foundation support. Working with Ragan A. Henry, a Philadelphia lawyer and businessman who served as treasurer of the Elderhostel corporation, they devised a plan to ensure the organization's financial integrity. The plan, approved by the Board of Directors in 1982, relied mostly upon voluntary contributions from Elderhostel alumni to the "Independence Fund."

From the start, the Independence Fund was wildly successful, netting $264,000 in its first year (1982–1983), compared to $114,000 in foundation support for the same year. The high rate of giving continued in 1983–1984, with a total of $323,000 in donations, allowing grant support to drop to $10,000. In its third year, 1984–1985, the Independence Fund netted over $500,000, and as a result Elderhostel was able to become fully self-supporting.* Time and resources were now freed from the work of writing grants and courting foundations, which allowed the organization to concentrate on its educational priorities.

*For a complete summary of the Independence Fund; grant support, and other budgetary figures, see Table 1 on pages 84–85.

The generosity of Elderhostel alumni continues today: roughly 20 percent contribute each year.[1] Every year's total sets a new record and there is no reason to believe the trend will diminish. In fiscal year 1991, the $2,000,000-mark was passed for the first time—109,637 people gave $2,070,000. Simple division indicates that the average gift is just less than $19. As in most facets of its organizational life, Elderhostel's financial strength is clearly in its numerous participants. It is reassuring to the staff and the Board of Directors that enrollment, both domestic and international, has continued to increase impressively during the recession of the early 1990s.

## INTERNATIONAL PROGRAMS

In 1980, foreign travel was becoming much more common for Americans and Canadians, a result of relative prosperity and relative international peace. In addition, environmental issues suggested the need for global cooperation, people-to-people initiatives were attracting attention, and Americans were becoming more culturally aware. "I think a lot of Americans have been embarrassed by the great attention paid to our military power, and by reports of 'the ugly American' abroad. We have wanted to see (and be seen) for ourselves," one participant said.

So in the spring of 1980 when two organizations independently approached the Boston office with proposals to create international Elderhostel programs, the time seemed right. The two organizations—Saga Holidays, Ltd., of England and Scandinavian Seminar (based in the U.S.)—were impressed by the flourishing response to Elderhostel in America. Both organizations believed they could provide the vehicle for even greater expansion.

Scandinavian Seminar is a small nonprofit organization located in Amherst, Massachusetts. Although the Seminar's primary focus is coordinating year-long study experiences in Scandinavian folk schools for American undergraduates, "the Seminar's contacts in the folk schools network, together with the schools' tradition of working with . . . older adults, made sponsoring programs with Elderhostel a natural extension of their mission."[2]

Saga Holidays had long been in the business of providing inexpensive holidays to British pensioners. They had extensive experience with one-week university-based vacations for "holiday makers," although without educational activities.

Both organizations had credentials that alone made them good candidates for collaboration, but the crucial factor in each case was a personal Elderhostel connection. Two members of the Scandinavian Seminar's Board of Directors were based at Hartwick College and were involved with Elderhostel there. Evelyn Bates, the Hartwick campus coordinator, and Peggy Anderson, wife of the deceased president of the college, made a convincing presentation to the national Elderhostel office. In the case of Saga Holidays, the connection was none other than Jerry Foster, one of Elderhostel's original "boys from Boston." Having worked with Saga when the organization first approached Elderhostel, Jerry left Elderhostel in order to help establish a U.S. office for Saga.

Working with these "friendly faces," Elderhostel soon began to offer education and travel programs abroad. In conjunction with Saga, programs were offered throughout Great Britain, Spain, Portugal, France, and Turkey. Through Scandinavian Seminar, courses developed in Norway, Sweden, Finland, Denmark, Greenland, Iceland, the Netherlands, Germany, Hungary, France, and Austria. Gradually, international programs became a larger and larger part of Elderhostel, and today there are programs in fifty countries, with 20,000 participants a year.

James Moses is Elderhostel's director of International Programs. There is a map of the world covering much of one wall of his office, with colorful pins stuck all over it representing existing Elderhostel programs. It is a striking visual representation of a truly worldwide educational network, as well as a reminder of the many unfulfilled opportunities.

A somewhat shy, soft-spoken person, Moses becomes animated when giving a tour of his map and the real world of educational opportunities it signifies. With a little imagination, one can see on the colored poster the tens of thousands of Elderhostelers scattered across the globe. There are thousands taking courses in England, Scotland,

Comparing an artist's conception of the original city of Kfar Nahum in Galilee to the ruins that remain, during a program in Israel.

Wales, and the Republic of Ireland. There are Elderhostelers studying in a course called "Amazonia" at the Museum Goeldi in Brazil. Others are studying "Hiroshima and World Peace" at the Peace Park and Peace Memorial Museum in Hiroshima, Japan; "Australian Reef, Outback and Rain Forest" under the educational supervision of the Capricornia Institute and University of Queensland in Australia; "The Kibbutz Experience" at the Kibbutz Kfar Blum in Israel; "The Arts of Polynesia" in Fiji, Tonga, and Western Samoa, offered in cooperation with Hawaii Loa College; "Crossroads of Civilization" in Istanbul, Ankara, Lappodocia, Ephesus, and Troy (in Turkey); "The Art of Mosaics" in Padua, Italy; "France Today" at the University of Paris/Sorbonne; and "Russian Culture and History" in a variety of universities in the former Soviet Union.

There are also hostelers in special interest programs such as a barge cruise in France; bicycle tours in England and the Netherlands; field center environmental studies in Great Britain; French-speaking only programs in France; home-stays in Bali, France, and India; mountain trekking in Nepal; study cruises in the Greek Isles; a safari in Kenya; and an educational visit to Las Islas Encantadoras in the Galapagos archipelago where one can walk among the giant tortoises, marine iguanas, Galapagos mocking birds, and the exotic blue-footed booby.

In all, the International Summer 1992 Catalog contains eighty-four pages of material devoted to the great variety of Elderhostel locations, courses, and arrangements. Participants in the summer courses in Lapland can tell you that, in all honesty, the sun never sets on the Elderhostel empire.

Most international programs are twenty-one days long and include one-week stays in three different countries or different areas of one country. Elderhostel coordinates the overall program, but programs are usually presented in collaboration with local universities and organizations whose faculty are native to the host country. This collaborative approach reduces greatly the administrative burden on Elderhostel itself, but choosing a suitable partner requires care.

'Subcontracting' overseas programs with independent organizations having specialized expertise in our destination countries is an alternative to trying to put into place a network of international offices of our own. A satisfactory partner must be one in which we have exceptional confidence, since we are authorizing them to set up programs that will be described in our catalogs as Elderhostel programs. In addition, international programs involve a lot of travel arrangements and each of our present partners is quite expert at working out various kinds of ground and water travel within the countries.[3]

Also, a number of American organizations with well-established international networks serve as facilitators for Elderhostel programs. Beginning with the original international partners—Saga Holidays and the Scandinavian Seminar—relationships have been established between Elderhostel and approximately two dozen organizations. For example, Trinity College of Hartford, Connecticut, handles programs in Italy; the Experiment in International Living undertakes programs in Switzerland, Germany, India, France, Mexico, and Japan; the College for Seniors provides programs in Australia and New Zealand;

and International Study Tours coordinates trips to Israel, Brazil, Egypt, Turkey, Argentina, France, Greece, and other locations.

The price of international programs includes round-trip airfare; all travel and transfers within each country; full room and board; academic instruction; course-related excursions and admissions fees; some evening entertainment; as well as limited accident, sickness, and baggage insurance. Although the price varies depending on the airfare from the U.S. gateway city to the destination, the figure for most programs is surprisingly reasonable. For example, a three-week Elderhostel trip to Great Britain is $2,375.* One can attend the program in India for $3,091; in Sweden for $3,096; in what was the USSR for $3,485; and in Israel for $3,357. As with the domestic programs, these are not trips to luxury hotels offering gourmet food. In the spirit of hosteling, the programs make use of dormitories, conference centers, and modest hotels; the food is simple and healthful. This is part of the trade-off for the comparatively low price—and it strikes most Elderhostelers as a very great bargain.

The academic program at international locations is similar to that in domestic institutions, often with an emphasis on local history and culture. There are daily classes, excursions and field trips, and evening activities. A typical program was the one the author attended in Thessaloniki, Greece, offered in conjunction with International Study Tours. The focal course, provided by Anatolia College, was entitled "From Zeus to Christianity." Activities included Dr. Dimitrios Pandernalis's lectures at the Dion archeological site, tours of Panorama and Thessaloniki, meals at colorful local restaurants, Greek dancing, and field trips to Pella and Meteora. The following week the entire group of hostelers continued the Greek experience by touring the Cycladic Islands on a vessel leased by Elderhostel, *Zeus III*. Lectures, on-site archeological visits, and tours of harbors and hill towns provided valuable insights into the culture and history of the Aegean region.

On the Thessaloniki program, as on all Elderhostel international

*Prices given here are for 1992 programs, calculated in United States dollars.

trips, classes are conducted in English. The reasoning for this is explained in the guidelines Elderhostel gives to foreign program coordinators.

Elderhostel's international programs are intended to provide an enriching academic experience that reflects the culture, customs, and traditions of the country, people, and region in which each program is hosted. The flavor of the program should be distinctly and uniquely representative of the host site. It is essential, however, since the majority of Elderhostelers will know nothing of the host country language, that all program staff interacting with the program participants in any substantial way be able to communicate well in English. This is the only required concession to Americanization to which Elderhostel must ask you to adhere.

This concession reflects a widely observed and frequently lamented national linguistic limitation, but it is a reality of foreign programs offered to Americans. According to international programs Director James Moses, almost all Elderhostelers are either Americans or Canadians, with the exception of a small number from Australia and Japan. However, there are an increasing number of inquiries from other countries about forming networks for elders so that they can participate.

The three-week length and institution-based format of programs such as the one described above are what set Elderhostel apart from most commercial travel. Many hostelers report that they are frustrated by commercial tours in which they see seven countries in eight days, live out of a suitcase, and leave without a single lasting impression of anything they have experienced. On Elderhostel programs, participants spend a full week at each institution. They have a chance to reflect on what they see, meet people native to the country they are visiting, and get a more in-depth understanding of a different country and culture. This more leisurely way of travel is an important consideration for elders. Bill Berkeley feels "The more reflective travel style is not necessarily appealing to the older adult because it is less demanding physically. Many of our coordinators overseas marvel at the physical vitality and energy of Elderhostelers. Rather it is more a testimony to the individual who at age sixty-five or so is interested in building in a significant way on earlier experiences or relating his or her own life experience to a new national or cultural context."

The opportunity for expansion of Elderhostel's international programs is virtually limitless. The Boston office receives as many as ten or twelve program proposals each week from travel agencies, nonprofit organizations, and universities. For years staff members actively followed up on every proposal, but recently the sheer volume of inquiries has made it necessary to put many of them on hold. The depth of interest can be attributed to many factors, according to Moses: Elderhostel has name recognition, the program is educationally superior to other opportunities available to elders, and the cost is almost always below anything in the marketplace. Moreover, the programmatic relationship with universities makes Elderhostel unique among international travel ventures.

The projected rate of growth in overseas Elderhostel raises questions and concerns for administrators and members of the Board of Directors. It is unclear, for example, what size and scope the international programs should take, and what balance should be maintained with domestic programs. If 20,000 people currently are eager to go abroad, is it important that Elderhostel make provisions for handling 40,000? There seems little doubt that such a figure is within reach if the necessary steps are taken to expand offerings and provide for those wishing to attend.

But focusing so much attention on international programs is not necessarily the most desirable use of resources. By their very nature, international programs are more difficult to administer than domestic programs: quality control is harder to monitor from such a distance; travel, meals, language, and lodging can all pose problems in a foreign setting; and participants are harder to reach in an emergency. Furthermore, because of fluctuating economic and political climates, international programs involve many more risks than domestic ones. Two recent situations highlighted this fact: the 1989 Tiananmen Square incident in China and the Persian Gulf War in 1991.

Elderhostel's China program had been launched in 1988, only after

A hosteler practicing her Mandarin Chinese in Hebei Province. (Photo courtesy of Elderhostel)

strenuous and protracted negotiations with government authorities. When the tragic events of June 1989 unfolded Elderhostel's Boston staff, as well as U.S. State Department and provincial officials, all worked overtime to evacuate the three hostel groups in China. The groups were removed without incident, and the next year Elderhostel programs in China were resumed, but the potential danger of the situation was clear to both staff and participants.

The hostilities in the Persian Gulf in late 1990 and early 1991 similarly "put Elderhostel 'to the test' in the planning and implementing of international programs."[4] Americans abroad were considered potential "moving targets" for terrorism and commercial travel decreased substantially. Elderhostel programs closest to the Gulf region had to be cancelled (those in Israel, Egypt, Turkey, and Greece), but most foreign programming was by and large unaffected. And though slightly fewer hostelers opted for international programs than the previous year, their numbers were still impressive. The first catalogue after the conclusion of the war states:

Because Elderhostelers travel to study and learn, many of them were more interested in observing and analyzing the world's current events from a 'ring-side' academic seat than they were concerned about the risks of doing so. With all of the conflict going on overseas last year, 20,292 Elderhostelers still chose to voyage to other lands in search of a learning adventure.*

As bold as hostelers may be, however, the Gulf War had a significant and sobering effect on Elderhostel's international programming. Perhaps for the first time it became apparent to the planners just how vulnerable a fifty-country network of programs is to outside influences.

Despite the real and potential difficulties of international programming, there is agreement among the leadership that the development of a worldwide presence is one of the most exciting and worthwhile aspects of Elderhostel. The greater distance and greater logistical hassle of international programs seems to correspond with an equally greater level of satisfaction among participants. The expanding horizon of international program development is well-expressed by one hosteler who spoke enthusiastically of his plans to "try my wings in all kinds of programs in the years ahead. I am excited to see all the opportunities and I wouldn't be surprised to learn from the next catalog that Elderhostel is reaching for Antarctica."

## ELDERHOSTEL CANADA

From the very first summer in New Hampshire, Canadians have been enrolled as Elderhostelers. The same change in attitudes that prompted the founding of Elderhostel in the United States was proceeding with equal fervor in Canada. In fact, as early as 1974, a program similar to the as-yet nonexistent Elderhostel was established in a vacant residence hall at Trent University, Peterborough, Ontario, by then-Dean of Arts and Sciences, Walter Pitman.[5]

The similar educational and social concerns on both sides of the

---

*This is the number of actual participants, but because many international programs are three weeks long, the total participant-weeks was 45,800, as shown in Table 1.

border provided the impetus for Canadians to first enroll in American Elderhostel, then for the development of Elderhostel programs in Canada, and finally for the establishment of a separate organization: Elderhostel Canada. Just as Marty Knowlton, David Bianco, Bill Berkeley, and Michael Zoob were of special importance in the creation of the American Elderhostel movement, so too has the Canadian organization had its own leadership. Several people played important roles, but it is generally understood that Robert H. Williston has been "the Bill Berkeley of Canada. He has made it all happen." *

Bob Williston is a solidly-built, energetic, self-described "former truck driver who got a Ph.D. in continuing and adult education from the University of Toronto . . . and who has had the good fortune to become a huckster, going out and promoting Elderhostel across Canada." When describing the role of Elderhostel in Canada, he brims with the friendly evangelism of someone who is thoroughly committed to his life's work. Williston graduated from the University of Guelph and served as assistant dean of social sciences until 1979 when he became assistant dean for continuing education at the University of New Brunswick. It was at this time that he remembers first becoming involved with Elderhostel:

In the late fall of 1979 two independent initiatives began in two very different locations in Canada concerning Elderhostel. At Humber College in the midst of the ever-growing city of Toronto, Remo Brassolotto was examining the possibility of leading a small number of Ontario institutions into the Elderhostel fold. In New Brunswick I was undertaking the same kind of assessment for the University of New Brunswick in Fredericton.

That fall, the Canadian Association for Adult Education brought Bill Berkeley to its meeting in Toronto. There was a great deal of excitement about the possibilities for Elderhostel, and the prevailing question was not *whether* but *when* Elderhostel would be coming to Canada. From this initial consultation there arose the proposal to appoint two Canadian representatives to the Elderhostel Board of Directors. Williston proposed Walter Pitman who had founded the Elderhostel-like pro-

---

*Comment made to the author by Walter Pitman, former Chair of the Board of Elderhostel Canada, Toronto, January 17, 1990.

gram at Trent University. His election was followed in 1982 by that of Lloyd Shaw, a Canadian businessman and community leader from Halifax.*

Beginning with the programs at Humber and New Brunswick in 1980, Elderhostel courses became regular offerings north of the border. From the perspective of Elderhostel Boston, these were essentially the same as other programs: administered and registered centrally through the Boston office, but carried out according to local strengths and initiatives. After the first year, however, the number of Elderhostel programs began to increase in Ontario and Atlantic Canada, and in 1981 programs were established in Quebec. As the programs and participation rates increased, there was a clear need to establish a separate Canadian office.

The office was opened in 1982 at the University of New Brunswick with Bob Williston in charge. By the next year, a separate Canadian catalog had been printed in French and English. With this mechanism in place, Williston took to the road to spread the word in the western provinces. Elderhostel would soon reach across all of Canada.

The catalyst for the establishment of Elderhostel Canada as a national program distinct from, yet closely associated with, America's Elderhostel, Inc., came in the form of a paper written in January 1982 by Douglas Myers, vice-chair of the Atlantic Provinces Association for Continuing University Education. Myers expressed his view that Elderhostel was "a splendidly compelling and effective educational programme for senior citizens." He wrote of its "elegant simplicity" and characterized it as an "idea with much promise for Canadian seniors and those involved in developing educational and social programmes to serve them." He held, however, that "to fully achieve that promise in Canada . . . it must develop into a truly national enterprise."

Myers called for further expansion throughout the provinces; a Canadian registration, catalog, and coordination system; and the creation of an independent Canadian Board of Directors. The American

*Shaw and Pitman served throughout the 1980s. Upon Shaw's retirement, E. Margaret Fulton, former university president and now an educational consultant, joined the Board.

leadership of Elderhostel was receptive to these suggestions and was committed to determining the best way of providing for the special needs of Canadians. This commitment is reflected in Bill Berkeley's President's report of October 20, 1982:

For 1981–1982, the Board approved a grant of $12,000 to the University of New Brunswick to establish a part-time Canadian office. This was done in response to a general feeling among the Canadian members of the Elderhostel family—a feeling expressed in many different ways by many different individuals—that somehow Elderhostel had to acknowledge the "Canadianness" of both institutions and participants from north of the border.

In 1986, Myers's original proposal came to fruition when Elderhostel Canada was incorporated as a nonprofit organization with Bob Williston as full-time director of a national office in Toronto. To assist in the creation of that office, the American Board of Directors of Elderhostel approved an allocation to the Canadian program of $75,000, an amount that Williston is proud to say was fully repaid by 1989.

That Elderhostel was flexible enough to help establish a sister organization, rather than viewing the Canadian initiatives as a threat, is appreciated by Pitman, Williston, and the others in Toronto. Pitman said, "Elderhostel has responded well and generously in a time of . . . nationalist fervor in Canada." It might not have worked out this way. The early success of the United States program, and the heavy personal involvement of those who established it, could have produced a protective attitude and an insistence that the Canadian interest be subordinated to Elderhostel Boston. Fortunately, however, the leadership in both countries was able to focus on the ultimate goal: the creation of opportunities for elders. This shared commitment overrode any national rivalries and an arrangement was created that recognized both the similarities between the two country's initiatives and their distinct needs for autonomy.

Now a well-established national organization with offices at 308 Wellington St., Kingston, Ontario, near Queen's University, Elderhostel Canada continues a strong relationship with Elderhostel, Inc., of Boston. Bob Williston attends the meetings of the American Elderhostel

Board, two members of which are also on the Canadian Board: Chair E. Margaret Fulton and Walter Pitman.* Similarly, both Bill Berkeley and Mike Zoob are members of the Canadian Board. Their official involvement will soon be phased out, but Berkeley will continue to attend meetings of the Canadian Board.

Much like its American counterpart, Elderhostel Canada operates in a decentralized manner, with directors for six regions: (1) the Atlantic region, with four provinces, (2) Quebec, (3) Ontario, (4) the three prairie provinces, (5) British Columbia, and (6) the Canada North region, consisting of the Yukon and the Northwest Territories. In Quebec, the Séjours Culturels Des Aînés Du Canada operates, according to Williston, as "a program within a program." Susan Adamson, director of Program Development, stresses that the regional directors provide much of the initiative that is needed in responding to growing demand for programs. Meeting as a committee, the directors work through the national office to plan, consider problems, and recommend policy to the Board of Directors.

With an annual growth rate of between 25 and 30 percent, Elderhostel Canada currently provides 13,650 participant-weeks of programming in cooperation with 260 institutions.† In the first years of Elderhostel Canada, the overwhelming majority of participants were Americans. In more recent years, however, 35 percent of summer participants and almost 75 percent of late winter/early spring participants are Canadian. Canadian programs are substantially the same as American programs, with a heavier emphasis on local history, culture, and customs. There are also uniquely Canadian initiatives, such as an experiment in which elder volunteers managed ten weeks of Elderhostel programming.

The Elderhostel Canada catalog appropriately characterizes the curriculum as "an intellectual smorgasbord of impressive proportions." The programs are offered on the campuses of colleges and universities

---

*In addition to Fulton and Pitman, the members of the Canadian Board are Michèlle Jean, a leading government official and author of the highly influential "Jean Report" on adult education; Dusty Miller, a woman who formerly was mayor of Thunder Bay; and Ann Frazer, an environmentalist who ran Elderhostel at the University of Victoria.

†Figures for 1990–1991.

Coffee break during a program in Canada North. (Photo courtesy of Elderhostel Canada)

as well as at inns, YMCA camps, conference and recreational centers, retreats and lodges. From urban centers such as Toronto, Montreal, and Vancouver, to the natural areas of the Atlantic and the prairie provinces, the programs are as varied in content as the geographic locations in which they are found. A small sampling of courses from the various regions suggests the diversity of the curriculum.

Atlantic region:
    "Inuit Crafts and History"
    "The Acadian French"
    "Newfoundland Culinary Delights"
Quebec region:
    "Saltdough Sculpture"
    "The Birds are Back"
    "Quebec—Its Literature"
Ontario region:
    "God's Peculiar People: the Amish, Hutterites, and Mennonites"
    "Political Parties in Canada"
    "The Brain and Behavior"
Prairie region:
    "Painting the Glorious West"
    "Native Experiences in Canada"
    "Alberta's Agriculture"
British Columbia region:
    "Trees—Guardians of the Earth"
    "500,000,000 Years in a Nutshell"
    "History of the Doukhobors: Who Are They?"
Canada North region:
    "Igloos to Microchips—A Generation of Change"
    "Exploring the Top of the World"
    "The Natural History of the Mackenzie Delta/Beaufort Coast"

In 1990, Elderhostel Canada and the American program cooperated on a special joint program developed by Bob Williston and New York State Director Doris Frazer. Participants studied the War of 1812, spending one week at St. Lawrence University in Canton, New York, and a second week at Queen's University in Kingston, Ontario. After the two weeks of study, the hostelers concluded that the very possibility of this cooperative program could be traced, in part, to the War and the subsequent neighborly peace. As is so often the case in Elderhostel experiences, the medium was the message.

The importance of the establishment of the Canadian program goes beyond the new opportunities opened for older adults. The Canadian story shows that the original idea of Elderhostel is adaptable even to a substantially different national circumstance. Older adults with the interests and motivation to stay active beyond society's expectations exist on both sides of the border. The success of Elderhostel Canada suggests that as a meaningful, challenging, and enjoyable solution to elders' needs, Elderhostel knows no boundaries.

# CHAPTER EIGHT

# ELDERHOSTEL
# TODAY

When a prospective Elderhosteler drops by the office to pick up a catalog today, he or she finds a sophisticated and automated operation. The comic chaos of earlier years has been replaced by a more settled scene in which staff members carry out their responsibilities efficiently and professionally. It is clear that, stressful as some days may still be, problems will be solved and organizational planning will proceed. The Elderhostel staffers have hundreds of thousands of people counting on them—and it shows.

The office at 75 Federal Street in Boston's business district provides a work environment that is something of a cross between an urban corporation and a collegiate academic department. The office is certainly corporate in its location and in the physical structure of the building. But the informal and democratic style of the place is in marked contrast to other corporations with annual budgets in excess of $10,000,000. Office doors are almost always open; first names are used, seldom last names or titles; most staffers, from the president and principal administrative officers to the telephone operators, wear sweaters, rarely ties or fancy blouses, and quite often sneakers. They dress up when it is important to do so, but apparently not often or eagerly.

It is understandable that the Elderhostel world is academic in style and practice; after all, it is an educational organization, and the great bulk of its relationships are with colleges and universities. The students may not be traditional college age, but the collegial spirit of learning pervades, and the educational mission is always the priority.

There are eighty full-time employees in the office, divided among eight departments: forty-two staffers work in the registration department (twenty-four of whom are phone operators), eleven in administration, seven in data processing, six in domestic programs, five in accounting, four in catalogues and publicity, four in international programs, and one in outreach. Somewhat ironic, given the nature of Elderhostel's clientele, is the fact that a majority of the staff are quite young. Many employees are college age because there is a tradition of hiring Northeastern University students during their co-op terms. These younger staffers enjoy having the opportunity to work with elders and often marvel at the hostelers' energy and spirit. The organization makes a point of arranging for staff members to visit programs at least once a year and the resulting encounters are an eye-opener for many employees. One staff member who recently visited a program commented, "It's tough to do an Elderhostel program—I'm not sure I could do it. You must get more flexible as you get older."

The driving force of Elderhostel today is the steady, but still remarkable, growth in enrollment. This growth is shown in Table 1. The dwindling foundation grant support and increasing Independence Fund lines reflect the Board's decision to become independent by 1985, as was discussed in the previous chapter. Perhaps most impressive is the fact that the Independence Fund grew from $264,000 in 1982–1983 to $2,072,000 in 1990–1991—an increase of almost 700 percent in just eight years.

The operating budget has risen at a similar pace, reflecting the greater administrative costs that accompany increased enrollments and inquiries. Because growth in enrollments has matched the rate of administrative growth, however, it has been possible to keep program cost increases to a minimum based on the rate of inflation.

Elderhostel has struggled throughout the years to deal creatively and effectively with growing demand, while at the same time plan-

TABLE I
*Enrollments, Operating Budgets, and Related Data*
(1974–75 to 1990–91)

| Enrollments | 1974–75 | 1975–76 | 1976–77 | 1977–78 | 1978–79 | 1979–80 | 1980–81 | 1981– |
|---|---|---|---|---|---|---|---|---|
| United States & Canada | | | | | | | | |
| Academic year | 0 | 0 | 0 | 0 | 225 | 300 | 2,000 | 7, |
| Summer | 200 | 2,000 | 4,800 | 7,200 | 12,775 | 20,300 | 31,400 | 40, |
| TOTAL | 200 | 2,000 | 4,800 | 7,200 | 13,000 | 20,600 | 33,400 | 47, |
| International | | | | | | | | |
| TOTAL | 0 | 0 | 0 | 0 | 0 | 0 | 3,600 | 7, |
| Grand totals | 200 | 2,000 | 4,800 | 7,200 | 13,000 | 20,600 | 37,000 | 55, |
| Total operating budget ($) | 0[b] | 0[b] | 0[b] | 141,000[c] | 412,000 | 611,000 | 741,000 | 1,135, |
| Foundation grant support ($) | 0[b] | 0[b] | 0[b] | 141,000 | 413,000 | 547,000 | 450,000 | 415, |
| Grant support as % of operating budget | N/A | N/A | N/A | 100 | 100 | 90 | 61 | |
| Independence fund ($) | | | | 0 | 0 | 0 | 0 | |
| Endowment fund ($) | | | | 0 | 0 | 0 | 0 | |
| Scholarships ($) | | | | 0 | 8,000 | 18,000 | 32,000 | 54, |

[a] The decreased international enrollment reflects program cancellations and participant withdrawal due to the Pers
Gulf War.

ning thoughtfully for the future. Berkeley, Zoob, Knowlton, and the Board of Directors have been committed to a belief that the organization should not be allowed to become whatever the pressures of growth might seem to dictate, but rather must constantly keep in mind the special characteristics of the program which spurred the growth in the first place.

During its evolution, Elderhostel has developed a somewhat schizophrenic organizational personality. The national office in Boston plays a crucial centralized role in registration, but programs are developed through a consciously *de*centralized system, on the theory that a headquarters in Boston is an inappropriate place to make decisions about programs that will be conducted throughout the country. With this philosophy in mind, there is an Elderhostel office in almost every state.[*]

[*]The exceptions are a single director for the six states in the New England region and directors in both northern and southern California.

| 982–83 | 1983–84 | 1984–85 | 1985–86 | 1986–87 | 1987–88 | 1988–89 | 1989–90 | 1990–91 |
|---|---|---|---|---|---|---|---|---|
| 12,800 | 20,000 | 26,800 | 33,300 | 48,250 | 60,000 | 83,500 | 109,000 | 129,800 |
| 43,900 | 46,800 | 47,600 | 53,950 | 55,750 | 59,000 | 59,750 | 54,350 | 61,100 |
| 56,700 | 66,800 | 74,400 | 87,250 | 104,000 | 119,000 | 143,250 | 163,350 | 190,900 |
| 10,300 | 13,200 | 21,600 | 24,750 | 38,000 | 43,000 | 46,750 | 52,650 | 45,800[a] |
| 67,000 | 80,000 | 96,000 | 112,000 | 142,000 | 162,000 | 190,000 | 216,000 | 236,700 |
| 64,000 | 2,142,000 | 2,488,000 | 2,926,000 | 3,582,000 | 4,545,000 | 6,159,000 | 7,617,000 | 9,186,000 |
| 14,000 | 10,000 | 0 | 0 | 0 | Total 1977–84: 2,090,000 | | 0 | 0 |
| 7 | 1 | 0 | 0 | 0 | 0 | 0 | 0 | 0 |
| 64,000 | 323,000 | 512,000 | 648,000 | 832,000 | 1,067,000 | 1,300,000 | 1,519,000 | 2,072,000 |
| 50,000 | 1,000,000 | 1,500,000 | 1,400,000 | 1,950,000 | 1,950,000 | 2,150,000 | 2,150,000 | 2,150,000 |
| 42,000 | 192,000 | 247,000 | 320,000 | 326,000 | 430,000 | 535,000 | 570,000 | 640,000 |

[b] Prior to the formal establishment of the Elderhostel organization. The first four years reflect summer enrollment. ginning in 1978–1979 the table reflects enrollments and other data on a total year basis.
[c] Half year.

The national office provides a detailed how-to manual for programs, which is more suggestive than prescriptive in its approach. Aside from this manual and the centralized registration activities, however, most of the work of running a program falls to the state offices. Each state office has responsibility for the recruitment of new Elderhostel institutions, the training of personnel who will administer programs at the campus level, the general support of existing programs, and maintenance of program quality in the state.

State directors are busy professionals who travel throughout their jurisdictions inspiring new programs, interpreting policy set by the national headquarters, and lending encouragement to campus coordinators. In many cases, the directors started out as on-site program coordinators and have been part of Elderhostel since the organization's early years. Peggy Houston, director for Iowa, and Bobby Wagoner in North Carolina are examples; both have been involved since their respective states' programs were initiated in 1977. Many state directors attempt to maintain daily contact with hostelers, but their administrative responsibilities rarely allow them the freedom to do so. Jiggs Gallagher, who as southern California director runs programs from Catalina Island to the desert, comments: "It takes a lot of time, energy, and consultation to develop and maintain big, diverse programs involving so many institutions." Cynthia Giguere, director of New England Elderhostel, has her hands full overseeing the entire six-state region.

Robert Conter, Arizona director, provides an example of the effect an aggressive and imaginative director can have on Elderhostel programming. In 1980–1981 there were only 448 participants in the entire state. By expanding to year-round operations, and by exploiting the state's many educational, geographic, and environmental assets, Conter managed to increase participation in Arizona to 17,921 nine years later. "Of course, the winter climate didn't hurt," Conter admits. Arizona now has seventeen "super-sites," a designation given to campuses that offer twenty or more programs per year. This represents more than a third of the forty-eight super-sites nationally.

In addition to the state directors, considerable responsibility is given to coordinators on each campus for the design and operation of their individual Elderhostel programs. Campus representatives decide what courses will be offered, who will teach them, what the weekly schedule will look like, and where the hostelers will be housed and fed. The operative concept is that each campus thinks of the program as truly *theirs*. Judy Goggin, Elderhostel's national program director, explains, "We try not to 'censor' courses or use too heavy a hand, because unless each institution feels the program is theirs, they won't have any investment in making it good." This philosophy can be traced directly to Marty Knowlton, who would not allow his brainchild to develop into "the McDonald's of older adult education"—a tightly controlled franchise operation in which predictability is the chief organizational priority. By contrast, each Elderhostel program is unique and distinctive, reflecting the character and philosophy of the host institution.

On the other hand, participant access to Elderhostel is facilitated by highly centralized, technologically complicated catalog production and hosteler registration functions that consume most of the financial and personnel resources of the national office. The idea is to treat all hostelers fairly and professionally.

Participant registration, at one time accomplished entirely by hand, is now a state-of-the-art operation. The majority of registrations are handled by mail, but a vast number are also accomplished by phone. Twenty-four trained operators work in organized shifts at computer terminals and telephones to handle over 150,000 calls each year. These calls and other inquiries are a year-round challenge to the registration staff. On average, the department receives 500 calls each day, and the mail could be measured in bushels.* Under the guidance of registrar Diann Bouthot, this unrelenting stream of communication is managed with a minimum of confusion. There is, of course, the occasional memorable phone call requiring special patience and tact—as when a woman called and insisted on knowing which of the thousands of courses had the most male registrants!

The greatest difficulty in the registration process is finding a match between space and demand. Some programs and locations are more popular than others, and at times applicants are frustrated when the program they want is already filled. Anne Maida, executive assistant to Bill Berkeley, recalls numerous instances when Elderhostelers, learning of her position, attempted to beg and bribe her to "get them in" to a certain program. Once she was even offered furniture in return for a program space, but she did not falter—equitable access to programs is a commitment Elderhostel takes very seriously.

In order to guarantee fairness in enrollment, the organization uses a lottery to designate spaces from all mail and phone applicants interested in a particular program. It works this way: the catalog is mailed from the printer in the Midwest during a two- or three-day period.

*This represents fewer than half of the total calls received by the entire Boston office, which in 1990–91 averaged 1,233 a day!

87

The actual registration is accomplished approximately one month after the catalog has been mailed, following a computer scrambling of all those who have responded. The organization believes that this provides equal access for everyone who acts relatively promptly on receipt of the catalog—a vast improvement over an earlier first-come-first-served policy, which penalized individuals whose catalogs were delayed by the uneven service of the post office.

The staff recognizes that sometimes an applicant may fail to survive this sorting process and be excluded even after two or more attempts to gain admission to a specific program. In order to partially address this problem, programs that have been listed in previous catalogs ("re-featured programs"), for which space is still available, are now filled on "an immediate first-come-first-served basis."

The catalog is the lifeline of the organization, and to most prospective participants it *is* Elderhostel. This publication explains courses, locations, arrangements, procedures, and the Elderhostel philosophy. Printing it costs almost half of the national organization's annual budget, but the catalog is extraordinarily important to the more than half a million people who receive it approximately ten times each year.*

The catalog is provided free to anyone who requests a copy. Copies are also sent to every public library and branch facility in the country—about 15,000 institutions in all. In addition to course descriptions and registration information, each catalog contains a brief history of Elderhostel, a statement of the organization's guiding philosophy, and other features, such as special messages from the president. Another crucial part of the catalog is *Between Classes*, the Elderhostel newsletter, which serves as a forum for updates and feature articles, often written by hostelers themselves. *Between Classes*, perhaps more than any other aspect of the publication, reflects the Elderhostel spirit. Witness the following description of a rock-climbing course:

*The cost of preparing, publishing, and mailing the catalog exceeds $4.8 million each year, approximately 45 percent of the 1991–1992 budget. The administration and Board are undertaking a review of catalog operations and plans are being made that will involve a segmentation of the mailing list, based on interest and need, so that not everyone will necessarily receive all catalogs.

"What's coming up at Elderhostel?" Hostelers peruse a catalog at Hampton University in Virginia.

"Half-way up I looked down, thinking, 'what in the world am I doing up here?'" recalls Californian Anne Eastwood of her first rock climb at Strathcona [British Columbia], "but there I was, and going back down would have been just as hard as going up. After crawling up from crack to crack, toe hold to toe hold, rappelling down on the end of the rope was a joy! The wide swings from the rock were like swinging on a grapevine."

Eastwood's encouragement to undertake the challenge came from a sign she saw posted over the kitchen door at the Strathcona Lodge: "Old Age and Treachery will Overcome Youth and Skill."[1]

Although most catalog "subscribers" are active or soon-to-be hostelers, a substantial number of older people receive the catalog even though they have not and do not plan to attend a program. These "armchair hostelers" simply like getting the catalog and reading the intellectual, geographic, and cultural features it contains. As one person put it: "I used to wait for the delivery of the Sears catalog or the one from L.L. Bean, but I don't get either one anymore. The Elderhostel catalog is what I live for now. That catalog has changed my life. Really!"

For several years the catalog was printed and mailed by local Boston firms. As the size, style, and production runs changed, there was no firm in Boston capable of handling such an enormous assignment. Eventually, it became necessary to go to the Midwest in order to find the expertise and production capacity that were needed. This area has the appropriate technology because Sears, Roebuck and Montgomery Ward are both based in Chicago and their catalog needs exceed even those of Elderhostel.

Even though the actual printing and mailing of the catalog is orchestrated in the Midwest, the mailing list itself is maintained and supervised in Boston. As of fall 1991 there were 569,321 names on the mailing list, which is kept on a highly sophisticated computer system and managed by three full-time employees.

It is not hard to imagine that many commercial, service, or public interest organizations would like to have access to over a half million older citizens who have demonstrated an interest in education and/or travel. Many organizations buy, sell, or trade mailing lists, but the officers of Elderhostel state unequivocally that their list is never shared. Bill Berkeley says, "we guard it like life itself."

Paul Duquette, who as Elderhostel's director of Operations designed and implemented the elaborate computer system, marvels at the contrast between Elderhostel's early years and its current existence. Duquette says, "Can you imagine it? This organization used to function with just typewriters, telephones, and three-by-five cards!"

In less than two decades, the changes have indeed been monumental. But although the index cards have been replaced by computers, the borrowed college office has turned into an entire floor of a building in downtown Boston, and what were initially 220 participants now number in the hundreds of thousands, Elderhostel today is, at the core, the same organization it was in 1975. Still present is the commitment to providing new opportunities for elders. Still present is the friendly atmosphere in which everybody is made to feel at home. Still present is the openness to new courses, new ideas, and new directions.

And still present—in a continual stream with no foreseeable end— are the Elderhostelers themselves, packing their suitcases for another adventure in Memphis, Milwaukee, or Madrid.

# PART II

# The Characters

# CHAPTER NINE

# SIX ELDERHOSTELERS:
# PORTRAITS OF
# ENGAGEMENT

In meeting and speaking with hundreds of hostelers over the past fifteen years, I have begun to recognize certain recurring themes. Hostelers differ tremendously in their individual personalities, and in their professional and geographical backgrounds, but their comments and anecdotes about Elderhostel experiences often sound common notes. They are likely to talk about what one hosteler called "life before Elderhostel, such as it was"; how they learned about the program; their initial uncertainty and nervousness about enrolling; their enthusiasm for the programs and teachers; and sometimes criticism of what they see to be shortcomings. They also speak about issues of special interest to elders: their concern to avoid an overdependence on television (the "wasted life syndrome," according to one elder); civil and economic rights for elders; and impatience with less venturesome peers. Invariably, there is much discussion of future Elderhostel plans, and, of course, grandchildren.

Most of these themes can be found in the following composite sketches, which are intended to provide a more in-depth and personal portrait of some of the many hostelers who have made Elderhostel as successful as it is. Though based on actual people, the sketches are true composites, written not to describe particular individuals, but rather to represent generally a few of the common "types" of hostelers. The six hostelers introduced here are Mary, a widow learning to cope again as a single person; Saul and Phyllis, confident "old pros"; Horace, a divorced man forced into early retirement; and Paul and Clara, a couple whose marriage is centered around books, ideas, and learning.

## MARY

Mary is an attractive, energetic sixty-nine-year-old widow. This is her seventh Elderhostel program, yet she is "still rather nervous" when she arrives, wondering just as on her first program whether she will be able to "get into the group and become one of them." However, it is not long before she seems at ease among the three dozen Elderhostelers who are present at the large university.

Mary's husband died a number of years before her introduction to Elderhostel after a "wonderfully successful marriage." Thrown back upon her own resources, Mary worked for a time in an undemanding job. Since she was not accustomed to being single, she was at loose ends, finding it difficult to become engaged in activities with other people. In just a short time, her job was no longer challenging enough to capture her attention and she began to search for other experiences to keep her occupied.

At this time a friend of Mary's who had recently attended an Elderhostel program told her about the organization. Mary was intrigued by the idea and wrote away for the catalog. After studying the material, imagining possibilities all across the country, she picked a program and began the registration process. But at the last moment, Mary "chickened out."

I guess I convinced myself I was too busy, or something—a rationalization, I now realize. You know, it is not easy to shake up your pattern of living, even when down deep you know you are not satisfied just going on the way you are. You think, well at least I am situated here, I have some friends, the kids are OK, and I can make it financially. Why run risks? What if I went to one of these programs and I wasn't happy? What if I got sick? What if I was embarrassed by being in a class again? So, I talked myself out of doing what I really wanted to do.

Mary continued to receive catalogs. Poring over these documents night after night she would "get all excited, pick one program, then

another," before her confidence would fade and she would put the catalog away. "Then finally, one time I up and sent in a registration!" Finally
committing herself to register in an Elderhostel program was an important step in Mary's growing independence as a widow. She remembers
"what a thrill it was! I really wanted to do more and make the most of
my remaining years. I thought, for crying out loud, I am in good shape,
I'm as bright as the next person, I'm really interested in learning. All
I was doing up till then was selling myself short. I was watching too
much television and hating myself for it."

Mary's first experience in an Elderhostel unit was a revelation. Years
earlier she had attended two years of college before dropping out to get
married and have children. After that experience she explains, "I had
always had reservations about my ability to handle abstract ideas." But
as an Elderhostel participant, the old doubts began to fade away. Mary
was able, to her own surprise, to ask questions and to participate in
class discussion. That first week of Elderhostel taught her that "I am no
dummy—at least I can do as well as most of the others in these classes.
I should add that it helps not having tests. I used to get all tense over
tests and not do as well as I knew I could."

Returning home after the program, Mary immediately opened up
the catalog and began looking at all of the offerings "with a whole new
notion that I could be a part of any one of those if I chose." Mary's
family was enthusiastic about her new adventures and encouraged her
in every way that they could. Her children lived in different parts of
the country and she began planning Elderhostel trips to take her near
their homes.

For her second Elderhostel experience Mary enrolled in a program
in the Midwest and went "like an old pro," completely prepared for the
experience. There was, however, one aspect of the program that came
as a complete surprise: a relationship with a fellow hosteler who had
been a widower for several years. The two had wonderful discussions
during the breaks between classes. On one occasion the man rather
informally asked Mary to walk with him to an ice cream parlor some
blocks away and she accepted, feeling "like a college coed having her
first date!" The relationship remained casual throughout and the two

new friends parted at the end of the trip. The courses had been as interesting as usual, but Mary says the realization that she was capable of enjoying such a relationship was the real lesson she learned on that Elderhostel program.

Mary now considers herself an "Elderhostel addict." She continues to explore new programs herself, in addition to preaching "the gospel of Elderhostel" to others she considers natural candidates for the experience. She feels Elderhostel can be especially beneficial for those, like herself, whose lifelong partner has died. She says:

It is hard to be a single person [again] after having been married. You aren't used to undertaking things just on your own. But Elderhostel is a wonderful way to get reengaged. You have a great group of people, an informal setting, good courses, and new friendships. Also, you're thrown with others, men and women, who have lost a spouse.

You know, when you get up in years a bit you tend to take on an attitude about yourself that seems to be mandated by society. You see yourself as "old," even though you know that you feel good and are able to handle new experiences. I remember particularly thinking about my own situation and realizing that clearly I did not have the energy and the physical power that I once had, but I marveled at the extent to which I was able to get around and to feel good about myself.

I tell my friends that every year can be a good one and that it is all a matter of developing the attitude and confidence that are necessary for new experiences. You know, I get the feeling that many of my friends have slipped into kind of a dream world. They go through their quiet lives, they watch lots of television, they have limited and unexciting things to do. I would argue with them that they ought to get up on their feet and see how much they can do. It is fun to challenge yourself when you are in your late sixties, just as it is fun when you are eighteen. It's all a matter of how you think about it, but I for one believe that it is possible to control a lot of your later life by just having the right kind of attitude about yourself. Elderhostel has helped me to see all of this.

## SAUL AND PHYLLIS

When Saul and Phyllis arrive on campus they park their van near the dormitory and go immediately to the lounge designated as the Elderhostel registration area. They are "old-timers," having attended over fifteen Elderhostel programs. They move forward confidently, introducing themselves to others as they arrive, with the combination of ease and ready excitement that one observes in college students returning from summer vacation.

There is little about the basic experience that will be strange to them—they have seen it all before. The only concerns they have are about the courses and instructors. Saul says:

You know we've had it all. Good courses and instructors, and not so good. Usually, it is just great and we come away feeling we have had a good experience and not sold ourselves short, if you know what I mean. We've done something worthwhile, learned something, met some people. It is so damned easy in our stage of life to settle down, accept what comes our way, stay in touch with the same few friends, watch TV and wait for it all to end.

Saul is seventy-four years old and aside from some minor heart problems is in good health. When he was growing up Saul's parents wanted him to be "some big corporate giant," but he went his own way instead. Taking a more low-key approach, he settled into school and an anonymous career. Looking back, however, he acknowledges some reservation about "what I've been able to accomplish in my life."

An accountant, Saul worked many years for a large firm; during the last ten years of his professional career he was "a solo private practitioner. Big deal!" When the time came, it wasn't easy for him to retire. He went through "some withdrawal pains," but had enough income to quit. Besides, he says, "I was tired of accountant's work and wanted finally to have some really new experiences."

Phyllis, "sixty-seven going on forty," is a lively, articulate woman. She was a sociology major in college who also took a teacher training program and fully intended to go on to graduate school. Marrying Saul changed those plans, but Phyllis did teach high school for several years after the marriage "and before the kids started coming like rabbits." Phyllis admits now to some regret that she was never able to return to teaching. "I really think I was good at it," she says. "I felt I was accomplishing something worthwhile."

Phyllis has always been a reader. She was reading a book, Saul says, "about a half hour before our first child was born." Saul believes that Phyllis was "an intellectually liberalizing influence in my life. She did a lot to broaden my thinking. You know, accountants don't tend to be broadly educated people."

Elderhostel is something Saul and Phyllis have discovered can help counteract their distinct feelings of regret. Just as the new experiences eased the pain of retirement for Saul, Elderhostel has allowed Phyllis to feel she is using her full intellectual capabilities again. Saul has seen its effects: "Elderhostel is right down her alley because she thrives on ideas and always wants to be on top of what's happening."

Furthermore, Elderhostel is something the couple can do and enjoy together. "The best thing about Elderhostel," Saul says, "is that we both get a kick out of taking courses, meeting new people, and going all sorts of places. All winter long we talk about what we did in Elderhostel last summer."

Based in part on their own experiences with Elderhostel, Saul and Phyllis believe strongly in the importance of forward looking attitudes for elders. Phyllis observes that they've "seen so many people who give up on themselves. They sink back into a state that is more and more withdrawn. Less and less activity and all of a sudden you realize that they are 'into being old.' That's a matter of attitude, you know. They are doing less than they're capable of doing, and less leads to less."

Saul and Phyllis are especially forceful in stating the case for "the rights of us senior citizens." Saul knows that "old people are people, after all. We have a lifetime of experience, we have learned something, and we have earned the *right* to be considered legitimate, rather than some kind of relic to be tolerated." Phyllis adds:

The older I've become, the more militant I've gotten. I'm a card-carrying member of the AARP, I write my congressman (not that it will do much good, but you've got to do it), and I keep up on legislation. It doesn't bother me one little bit that older people are seen by some to be a selfish political force that is trying to protect what's good for us. I tell my kids, I'm all for you and other younger people, but I'm entitled, too.

At this Elderhostel program, Saul and Phyllis are "an item." They are always on time, ready to go, full of spirit and good humor. In class, Phyllis is especially prepared to ask questions and challenge ideas. She is popular among the other hostelers, one of those people who always "make things happen."

During the course of the week, Saul and Phyllis trade stories with their fellow hostelers, about their lives, their children, and plans for the future. They poll others about Elderhostel programs they haven't yet attended, and recommend the courses they have found especially interesting. It is ever apparent that they are pointed forward, always looking toward experiences yet to come.

This is not to say they don't acknowledge that there are limits to their remaining years. Their energy isn't what it used to be, there is more "unscheduled napping," and "joints and muscles seem sometimes not to have heard that we have big plans for them." But, they are determined to keep at it and "to see what is in store for us." Phyllis reflects: "We aren't kidding ourselves. We know we're kind of old, but my God, what fun it is to go on and to do all of these things. Saul likes to say that we'll probably die at the registration table in some Elderhostel program. And I say, 'what a way to go!' "

## HORACE

"It was one of the most discouraging days of my life," Horace recalls. "When these companies make decisions to reduce the workforce, they just up and do it. You get caught in the situation, even though you have worked most of your whole career for the company and think you've got maybe five years left." We are sitting in the lounge of a conference center at a large university. Horace has come here for a week of Elderhostel, a new experience he hopes will help him handle the sad after-effects of his recent forced retirement. He was shocked at the difficulty in making the transition:

I know now that I didn't prepare for retirement, but really the big problem was having to adjust to a sudden, unexpected, early retirement. I'm sixty-two now.

I was divorced about a dozen years ago, but somehow not even that hit me as hard as learning that I was one of those who was going to be retired early—let out to pasture, as they say.

Horace had spent about thirty years with the same manufacturing company, which he had joined shortly after attending one year of college. One of approximately a thousand employees, he was a steadfast member of the team, and his loyalty was rewarded with promotions. He advanced from office work to positions of increasing responsibility, culminating with his appointment as assistant vice-president in charge of a number of purchasing and supply operations. Horace married a fellow employee, but a divorce followed fairly soon after. His job was his life. He remembers, "Most of my friends were in the company. I didn't go out a lot."

Although he had often considered further collegiate education, and had completed three extension courses in business, Horace "just didn't seem to want it badly enough. And besides, I was doing well in my work and I needed the money." However, he became connected with a local university through its athletic program because, he explains, "I went to most of the home football and basketball games. I guess you could call me a booster. I bought season tickets, went to some of the athletic dinners, and even contributed a few hundred dollars a year to the booster fund. Most of this was after my divorce, and it helped me get my mind off my troubles."

In a bulletin sent to alumni and special friends of the university, Horace read about Elderhostel. He was apprehensive about getting involved, but desperate to stay active after his retirement. Finally he sent for a catalog, which ". . . was a big surprise. I had no idea that there were so many programs. Frankly, there are so many that it is difficult to decide what to do. But, I chose this one because our teams play this school and it isn't too awfully far away. I thought it would be fun to be on the campus of the place we beat so often!"

In the conference center lounge, Horace reflects on his first Elderhostel week. He finds the people in the program interesting and the courses generally worthwhile, but he is keeping a protective distance from the experience. He is bothered by the fact that there is so much discussion, "some of it by people who would rather talk than think and listen." He seldom participates, preferring to "learn what I can and just get my mind off myself."

Horace's bitterness and protectiveness are understandable, especially when he speaks of the "system that can suddenly bounce people out of jobs that they have been devoted to for so long." He is struggling with his identity as an older person, just becoming conscious of his position in the movement for elders' rights. "I surprise myself with how strong I have become about this," he remarks. "I am ready to support legislation of some kind, but I can't say what kind."

When asked how he might have prepared better for life after retirement, Horace says:

Probably I could have done something to get ready, but I am not sure what. Golf or something. But I am enjoying the athletic programs and that helps. No doubt it would be good for me to try another Elderhostel. In fact, I have been toying with going to a program in Indiana. I've got a cousin there I haven't seen in years. I think it might be fun. We don't play Notre Dame, but I've always wanted to see the stadium.

## PAUL AND CLARA

You see them walking together, close but not touching, synchronized in gait and manner as if their long marriage has made them function as one. In their early seventies, and both a bit unsteady on their feet, Paul and Clara admit that there are some days when they "just want to sit around and do nothing." But here they are in England, keeping up with all the rest of the hostelers.

Paul and Clara are readers. They carry books in their suitcases. Paul says:

You may surmise from my appearance that I carry with me more books than clothes. Both my books and my clothes are reasonably clean, you understand, but there is no doubt about my priorities. Clara complains sometimes that since I retired I often get started reading in the morning and forget to get dressed.

Photographing rare plant species in the ecologically unique Burren of Ireland.

But I have a very clear view concerning retirement. It is a time in life when I control my lifestyle. If I want to sit around all morning in my pj's drinking tea and reading, then I can do just that. Clara's a reader too, but she seems to need to get properly dressed before picking up a book.

Before retirement, Paul had worked for the federal government in a job requiring a great deal of travel and many lonely nights in far-away hotels. Books were his defense against loneliness and his "access to sanity, learning, and beauty in this all too sordid and complicated world."

Clara is a bright, talkative woman who always wanted to go to college. But a week-long marriage to a soldier during World War II, and the son she had to raise alone as a result, dictated different plans.

She and Paul met in the library of a small western town where they were both working in the 1950s. "For our honeymoon we threw a couple of dozen books in the trunk of Paul's old Plymouth and went off to a campground in the Rockies. For two weeks we read, hiked, and made love—not necessarily in that order."

Books brought them together and books have continued to dominate a long and satisfying marriage. Clara explains, "We don't just read, we talk about what we read. Sometimes we argue about what we read. We trade books, sneak books away from each other, and give each other books for presents. Paul knows that when I give him a book for Christmas it's usually because I want to read it."

When a friend told them about Elderhostel, Paul and Clara went immediately to the library and pored over the catalog. Two days later they signed on for a week in Canada. "That was one of the best weeks we ever had," Clara recalls. "We met others our age who were from all over creation and we just had a marvelous time talking and talking. The course was interesting and we came away with a wonderful reading list about Canadian life, geography, and culture."

Six months later they were again in an Elderhostel program, this time in France. Paul had been to France many times during his years with the government and he relished introducing Clara to familiar sights: "Travel abroad was old stuff to me and I had thought I'd never want to leave the United States again. Years had passed, however, and I found it was exciting to go abroad with Clara, and to do so in the company of others who were interested in learning."

For Clara, Elderhostel provides some of the academic experiences she missed by not attending college. She takes great satisfaction from feeling comfortable in the classroom setting, and from participating in the give-and-take of class discussions.

Paul and I are used to reading and talking about what we read, but it is fun to be involved with others in thinking about issues. We both have found a new dimension to our lives by participating in Elderhostel. Many older people we know have stopped thinking about issues in a fresh way. I suppose they have lived long enough to have developed a habit of just extending old judgments, carrying their views and their prejudices into whatever problems they face. But Paul and I like to think about things in new ways. The world is changing and old and familiar points of view are not enough anymore. Recently in an Elderhostel program the subject of world population came up. It was clear to me that some people in the class had not quite grasped that there are big tides running and that we've got to face up to the population question.

I'm largely self-educated, but it tickles me to feel comfortable in an Elderhostel class and to try out ideas on other people. I'll always be grateful that we found Elderhostel and so many wonderful people who are intellectually alive. It makes living in our little town lively for us, instead of dull. Not even books are enough. You've got to get out and among 'em!

Late in life, Paul and Clara certainly have succeeded in getting "out and among 'em." They have moved along from program to program and have introduced a number of their friends to Elderhostel. Paul says, "I'll bet it would be hard to find another little town that has produced so many hostelers. We ought to get a discount!"

# CHAPTER TEN

# ELDERHOSTELERS

# WRITE ABOUT THEIR

# EXPERIENCES

I n telling the story of Elderhostel I have quoted dozens of participants and have sketched six composite hostelers in greater detail. A different perspective is provided, however, in accounts written by participants themselves. Elderhostelers tend to be extroverted, verbal people, so perhaps it is not surprising that many are inclined to write about what has happened to them during the program. The Elderhostel office files contain dozens of articles by participants that have been published in newspapers and magazines across the country.

These Elderhostel accounts most often chronicle the excitement of newfound friendships, the joy of learning, and the challenges of travel. Occasionally hostelers write to vent their complaints about the quality of the food, the difficulty of gaining admission to popular programs, or the inconvenience of shared bathrooms. Sometimes Elderhostel is not the subject at all, but rather a touchstone for other topics. One participant was inspired to write and publish a murder mystery set at an Elderhostel program! *

What follows are excerpts, and in some cases full reprints, of representative writings by Elderhostelers. All but two of the pieces are reprinted from *Between Classes*, the Elderhostel newsletter (volume and number citations are listed with each). The first brief commentary is by

---

*Anne Baker, *No Tears for Harriet* (St. Petersburg, Fla.: Quiett Publishing, 1989). Fortunately, the crime was entirely a product of the hosteler's lively imagination; Elderhostel's history offers no known precedent for such a plot.

two "Originals," people who attended the initial summer of programs in 1975.

## RECOLLECTIONS

*by Edward and Marion Ennis*   (vol. 3, no. 1)

Thank you Elderhostel! We've carved linoleum; found a beaver dam; climbed around mountains, temples in India, a Roman bath in Wales, over the remains of an amphitheater in England; sailed on Loch Lowan in Scotland; ridden in an ancient outrigger canoe in a bay out of a palm-shaded lagoon near Kuna, Hawaii; and found giant pine cones at 7,000 feet in Idlewild, California.

Ed played jazz piano with fellow students at two Elderhostels at Chapel Hill, North Carolina, and in shows on Friday nights at many other Elderhostels. We've enjoyed cookouts at programs in Amherst, Massachusetts, and Lyndon, Vermont, and a luau in Hawaii. We've sat on the lawn drinking coffee at Cambridge University, danced the English dances and sung Welsh songs, drunk Scottish "scotch," and become hula experts. We learned to wear a sari and eat with our fingers in India, and invited half of the people home. There they venerate older people, so when we become old we'll visit India again.

The classes and Elderhostel weeks have become better as leaders, coordinators, and instructors have learned that Elderhostelers are positive-thinking, energetic people, and as we have showed them what we really think, feel, and want to do.

So, our thanks to you, Elderhostel leaders—and to everyone we met at the great tenth anniversary celebration! At last we were V.I.P.'s, Hurrah!

## AN INSPIRING WEEK AT NOTRE DAME

*by Clifford Massoth*   (vol. 6, no. 1)

A week after my program at the University of Notre Dame in Indiana, looking back, I have an overwhelming memory: it was simply wonderful. Surprising, too. For one thing, Director Kathy Sullivan was a young, bright woman who introduced herself to us by proudly tapping her slightly bulging stomach to show us her first child-to-be. Secondly, I was not prepared for the beauty or the size of the campus. The third pleasant surprise was the campus dining service. Imagine— cherry, apple, peach, rhubarb, and pumpkin pies for any meal! As a man who does his own cooking, I was delighted. By Thursday, with an iron will, I told myself "only one piece of pie today!"

I chose Notre Dame mainly because of the three courses offered: "Human Evolution: Prehistory or Poetry?", "Pascal on Faith and Reason," and "Wet- and Dryland Aerobics." How lucky can you be? Each was better than I had any reason to hope for. Our two Ph.D.'s, I heard, had been picked by the freshman class as favorites. If so, then the students had made no mistake. Dr. James Ellis was middle age, bulky, balding, bronzed. He made anthropology electrifying. I had read Loren Eiseley's *The Immense Journey* (and have reread it since my return) so the subject was one reason for choosing Notre Dame. The school, free of cost, sent Eiseley's *The Firmament of Time* in time for us to read before the course. Dr. Ellis, in his five 8:30 A.M. lectures, must have saved all of the jewels of his college classes to throw before us because he was simply inspiring. He made mankind come alive, showed us how our species is swiftly, and not wisely, changing the world. His illustrations were stunning: "We Americans are using 75 percent of the world's calories." (And I didn't want to make him a liar as I passed down the cafeteria line.) "We have exported the sweatshop around the world." "Ninety-five percent of medical science is directed to the aid of the wealthy." He gave a stunning lecture on the gene pool. "Some mules are fertile." (I didn't know that!) "Nature keeps experimenting, and fortunately most of her mutations are self-destructive." He spoke of the knotweed which grows between rows of corn, and on which farmers spend millions to poison—yet the weed has more food value than corn as animal feed, and ground up with corn makes a more nutritious feed.

Next, Sandy Vanslager, young and lively, put us through our paces in the aerobics class. The first day, at practically a dog trot, she led us around St. Mary's Lake. On subsequent days we were in the pool in hard-working aerobics. With my damaged ticker I was concerned, but during the next three days I felt great, even though part of the class dropped out.

In a different way, Dr. Tom Morris was equally outstanding. A younger man, a six-footer with a shock of long black hair, he threw himself with enthusiasm into interpreting the philosophy of Blaise Pascal, the seventeenth-century Frenchman who combined scientific brilliance with theology and philosophy.

Dr. Morris operated from a disadvantage: His class went to the swimming pool before lunch and came to him after lunch, and eyelids were heavy—as often was the subject. But Dr. Morris came at us swinging, throwing key thoughts on the screen with enormous enthusiasm, explaining the profound thoughts of Pascal. His one session on Woody Allen (!) was exceptionally fine. Dr. Morris had made a film strip of scenes from Allen's many movies, showing the comedian wrestling with some of the difficult spiritual problems of modern society. I can understand why the Notre Dame football team attends his classes.

The campus and its striking buildings and splendid collection of trees was a wonderful backdrop to the classes. I walked over much of the big campus, including a walk around St. Joseph's Lake which lay below my third-floor window. I saw the lovely Moreau Seminary and its handsome sanctuary. One evening, classmate Marie Green of Cleveland showed me the grotto at night behind beautiful Sacred Heart Church, with its great boulders and the many candles flickering in the night air, and the bowed heads of the kneeling worshippers.

Besides our three daily class sessions and the lovely campus, we had lively events each evening. On the first night, to help us to become acquainted with each other, Kathy Sullivan demonstrated her ability to remember all of our names and our pet peeves. On another night, Tom Morris brought his beautifully crafted black walnut dulcimer, made in the Blue Ridge Mountains, and entertained us royally.

The next night we had group singing, which I, a four-year tenor in

Crane Tech's glee club, thoroughly enjoyed. The last night brought a lively outdoor dinner, followed by a gathering in the lounge which was attended by our three instructors and their spouses. Both Dr. Ellis and Dr. Morris were good musicians and we all sang. And old grandpa here, after a lifetime in sales and public relations work, got out his string of well-honed jokes, which seemed to go over well. A joyous evening.

The quality of the program and the beauty of the campus was so magnificent that I felt I was in heaven. Had to tell someone! Notre Dame—I won't forget you!

## LETTER OF APPRECIATION

*by Innes Browne*\*

I returned home on August 8th after a superb Elderhostel program at Arctic College, Yellowknife campus, at which I learned a great deal about the Northwest Territories.

The day we registered we were each given a box of fruit, a mug with the Arctic College crest on it, a lapel pin of the College crest, and a second lapel pin in the shape of the yellow knife that was used by miners to open dynamite cases. It was made of copper because an ordinary steel knife could cause an explosion and death to the miners. This lapel pin was given to each of us by the mayor of the City of Yellowknife. Another gift was an item often stolen in earlier years: the Northwest Territories motor license plate in the shape of a polar bear!

There were many excellent and informative speakers during the week's program, representing several professions and various cultures. A panel of those marrying outside their own culture spoke very freely of the problems, how they were overcome, and the effect [of such inter-marriage] on children. We had several Déné and Métis speakers and spent a delightful evening in a Déné encampment where they taught us how to make and cook bannock (unleavened flat bread made with oatmeal or barley meal) over a campfire.

---

\*From a letter sent by Mrs. Browne, of North Vancouver, British Columbia, to the central office of Elderhostel Canada, June 23, 1990.

Elderhostelers get a close-up look at early Christian art at a museum in Greece.

The coordinators, Deborah Simpson and Sandy Osborne, as well as John, Deborah's husband, took us all on many field trips about the countryside and tours of interesting buildings, such as the Cultural Heritage Museum and the Legislative Assembly. At the courthouse we saw carvings by a Canadian judge depicting Inuit and Métis trials for murder or breaking conservation laws and the correlating judgments, based on ancient Inuit customs.

An unexpected treat was to attend a gathering in the local park to greet the Governor General of Canada, the Hon. Ray Hnatyshyn, on his first official visit since his inauguration. He spoke to many of us and several had a picture taken with him.

The meals were very generous, with many selections always available. There was plenty of fruit and vegetable salads, and I enjoyed the specialties of caribou stew, musk ox burgers, and Arctic char.

Our final evening was a boat cruise on Great Slave Lake to an island where we had a barbecue of Arctic char and were presented with our graduation certificates from Arctic College and a certificate admitting us to the North of 60° Chapter, Order of Arctic Adventurers.

I have only mentioned a few of our many speakers, trips, tours, and activities. The coordinators and chef of the cafeteria went out of their way on many occasions to give us a wonderful welcome and a superb learning experience.

Because I was already in the North, I flew up to Inuvik after our program ended and spent three days there. Now I'm giving thought to seeing the eastern Arctic, hopefully on Baffin Island if there's an Elderhostel course available next year!

## TO GREECE LIKE PILGRIMS TO A FEAST: AN ELDERHOSTELER'S TWO-WEEK ODYSSEY

*by Beverly Shaver** (vol. 5, no. 2)

We came together, as the wildflowers burst into bloom in early May, on a two-week quest—to know and understand Greece: that great civilization, that spiritual and mental inheritance that has never been surpassed, and which has left an indelible stamp on the art and thought of the Western world. And after a few days in Athens, it was evident to all thirty-four of us that International Study Tours, Ltd., our guide, mentor, and "in loco parentis" for this Elderhostel program, was an exacting if enthralling sponsor. This was indeed an experience for "those who seek knowledge and understanding beyond the usual sight-seeing tour," as the brochure cautioned, and, sure enough, it had attracted a group with sunlit minds and adventurous, contemplative spirits.

We trooped each morning through the unleashed pandemonium of Athenian streets the few blocks to the tranquil haven of the Hellenic-American Union where a series of able historians, political scientists, and sociologists took us reeling, entranced through the great ages of

*A writer from California, Beverly Shaver currently serves on the Elderhostel Board of Directors.

Greece. We identified the crucial differences between the Greeks and the Spartans: the latter militaristic, laconic, intolerant; the former preoccupied with the arts, politics, and commerce. We traced the complicated course of the Peloponnesian War. (Plague resulted from the siege; much of the history of mankind can be explained in medical terms, we were reminded.) There was exploration of the period when a victorious Rome was gently conquered by defeated Greece through the latter's culture and the power of its ideas; of the dawn of Christianity and the conflict between the new moralistic ideology and the old Hellenic philosophies. We learned about the era of oppressive Ottoman rule, when the Turks took able young Greek boys and made warriors of them. Thirty thousand young Greeks died on Ottoman ships. We heard about modern Greek dualities and the need for greater political maturity. "We have finally understood that we need to be less passionate, more moderate, more reasonable, less dominated by one individual," thundered Professor Zaronis.

Luncheons back at the comfortable, but hardly palatial, Esperia Palace on Stadiou Street were the scene of swirling discussions, arguments, commentary on the morning's topics as we chewed our way through the wholesome if not gourmet four-course meals. "Too much food," was the frequent cavil. "The Greeks are killing us with hospitality!"

"Well, now, you don't have to eat it all," chided our patriarchal maitre'd.

"But we belong to a generation that always had to clean its plates," we protested.

Then, after what always seemed the briefest of digestive intervals, we assembled at the waiting bus for the afternoon's ramble. Ours was a group uniformly observant of the beatitude that blessed are the punctual. No one was ever late. We ranged widely over the city and countryside, grateful that it is still possible in overcrowded, horrendously congested, polluted Athens to see in relative comfort the treasures that have captured the imagination of the world. Our local host, George Tsilides, and our patient, earnest young escort, Gregor, had arrangements and operations down to a finely honed science.

We sat mute, awed, in our marvelously varied sun hats and dark glasses, on three great fallen blocks of pentelic marble as we looked up at the Parthenon, pink in the smoggy afternoon haze. Later, we hung over the railing at Corinth, mesmerized by the slow passage of boats below as they cleared—by inches—the concrete walls of the seventy-five-foot-wide canal, making their way between the Aegean and Ionian seas. We strained to see, high in the hills, the Corinthian Acropolis where, in the last centuries B.C. sailors threw riotous orgies while their ships were being provisioned in port. "I'll bet there were a lot of big delays in provisioning those ships," quipped our group wag. We traveled to nearby Kesariani with its vine- and flower-covered monastery, the tranquil gardens belying the bloody World War II executions of whole villages in the vicinity [by the] Nazis.

In the villages of the countryside, in the street markets of Athens, we were struck again and again by the contrasts between our energetic, lightly wrinkled, pleasantly frosted sixty- and seventy-year-olds in jumpsuits and flight jackets, and our bent, wizened, black-garbed counterparts. How much is nutrition, how much is exercise and shielding from the sun, how much is the American obsession with youth, we wondered. (My lithe, blonde, sixty-eight-year-old roommate always took the hotel elevator to the seventh floor and then bounded the last two flights on foot—"for my cardiovascular system.") The Greek elders were a chastening reminder of the blessings of living in a prosperous, industrialized society.

Late in our Athens week, young, brooding Greek men suddenly appeared on chairs at the end of each corridor in our hotel. These were round-the-clock sentries in preparation for a Communist Party Congress convening the following week. The more timid members of our group were uneasy, uncertain whether the menace was greater from surveillance forces or the imminent proximity of "evil empire" folks. But the only mildly exciting episode occurred as we waited in the hotel lobby for the bus on our last day. Our smallest and eldest member was suddenly confronted by a hulking Greek security officer, who, deadpan, was wearing her lost Elderhostel I.D. badge pinned to his red tie and restored it to its fluttering owner with a bow and a flourish.

The Hellenic-American Union held a wine and cheese "graduation" party for us at the end of the week and awarded us all with "certificates of achievement." We shall treasure them and the so relevant words of Homer quoted by the director that evening: "Dear to us ever is the banquet and the harp and the dance and changes of raiment and the warm bath and love and sleep."

Inheritors of the classic tradition, who were we to quarrel with such a prescription for the celebration of life or with the questing mind which refuses to believe there are any bounds to reason?


## ON CAMPUS AND OVER 60

*by Susan L. Peck* *

In the course of a three-week trip to Australia this year, forty individuals aged sixty-plus coalesced into a group resembling nothing so much as a bunch of sorority sisters and fraternity brothers. The transformation was effected by a Boston-based organization called Elderhostel, which specializes in study trips for adults sixty and over at colleges around the world . . .

During our three-week trip we encountered koalas, emus, and kangaroos. We tried to make a bunk bed consisting of a slab of wood covered with slippery plastic. We saw a quarter-moon in reverse, and tried to shear a sheep. We lived four people to a trailer, paid 20 cents for a three-minute hot shower that invariably turned cold after one minute, and made do with only one small, thin, nonabsorbent towel a week.

The adventure began at the Qantas terminal in San Francisco airport, where six Elderhostel groups of forty people each were bound for various destinations in Australia. Each group was assigned a different color on its name tags; ours was yellow.

After the fourteen-hour flight, overfed but still ambulatory, we were met on our arrival in Sydney by courteous tour representatives who

*Excerpted from an original article in the *New York Times*, September 21, 1986, p. 12. Copyright © 1986 by The New York Times Company. Reprinted by permission.

guided us through the complexities of customs and luggage retrieval and onto special buses for the ride to the Sheraton Wentworth. . . .

For the majority, it was to be an incomparable experience; for a few, impossible. As we cautiously surveyed each other at [our] first meal together, tidbits of information were exchanged, and one thing soon became apparent: We were a group of alert, intelligent individuals, most of whom had enjoyed (or still pursued) lives of accomplishment—doctors, nurses, teachers, and more. We . . . ranged in age from about sixty to eighty-four; there were nine married couples, twenty-one single women, and one single man.

On Sunday morning each group set out for the locale of its first week. The Yellows traveled only to the outskirts of Sydney, arriving by bus at the gates of the Women's College of Sydney University, a vast enclave of stone walls, rolling greenery, and ancient buildings. We were now being shepherded by our group leader, Felix Goward, a twenty-three-year-old Tasmanian who was every mother's dream of a son (or son-in-law): he was intelligent and handsome, with a good sense of humor. He soon became alert to our every need, our moods, and our few complaints.

The basics of life at the Women's College could politely be called austere: single dormitory rooms, except for couples traveling together; coarse linen and blankets piled on each unmade cot bed; a desk with a rickety chair, some built-in shelves. Just adequate, yet so different an environment for us that it seemed rather charming.

As we wildly attempted to unpack in the allotted ten minutes before morning tea, we heard a sort of shriek from down the hall. Rushing to the aid of the noisemaker, I found the tenant of the nearby room (a retired professor of English) jumping up and down with glee as she pointed and cackled. Firmly glued to the wall was a life-size, very young Clark Gable, displaying his dimples and clad in what can only be described as a zoot morning suit. Finding such a fine example of Americana so far from home was a delight, and the tenant of the Gable Room soon had more drop-ins than she could comfortably handle.

Our week at the Women's College passed fleetingly, even frantically, with mad dashing about to our various activities, all supervised by two college administrators. . . . The classes were all excellent and taught in a manner that allowed for discussion, with an emphasis on the history, government, and mores of Australia . . .

We were given free bus tickets for the week, allowing us to jaunt about on our own in Sydney, get lost, and chat with any Australian who looked approachable. Through the college many of us attended the opera one evening; surprisingly, our last-minute seats were some of the best in the house.

The dining hall at Women's College was always crowded. The self-service operation became a jolly "search and seize" mission, as we tried to pinpoint the ever-changing location of the viands. Orange juice seemed most inclined to move, frequently disguising itself in a large milk can accompanied by a soup ladle. If you wanted eggs you put your initials or some pertinent hex mark on a raw egg and carefully dropped it into a communal pot full of simmering water. Timing as well as retrieval was an individual responsibility. Food was becoming increasingly important to us, and counting our morning and afternoon "tea" breaks, most were now eating five meals a day.

The only real cloud in our sky was a bronchial flu virus that struck suddenly and capriciously throughout the three weeks. Felix took patients to the doctor, secured medicines, brought meals, got lamps and bedside tables for the needy—a model nurse and worrier.

The headquarters for the second week of our trip was the Orange Agricultural College, about 200 miles inland from Sydney. . . . Aboard a special bus . . . we settled in for a long trip, punctuated, of course, by a tea stop, a ceremonial endeavor involving huge pots set to boil over an outdoor fire. We stopped at a public park inhabited by casually wandering emus and kangaroos, which were very curious and seemed very friendly. The emus were imperious and cranky; the kangaroos seemed to manifest a need for nuzzling. Hours later, sodden with food and the long journey, we arrived at Orange Agricultural College, a modern complex nestled into the countryside.

We were welcomed by the program administrator who warned us about the poisonous snakes in the area. If bitten, he advised, we were

Elderhostelers explore the amazing rock formations in Australia.

to simply catch the snake so that the authorities would know which antitoxin to administer. I never quite categorized that gentleman's humor.

The lodgings at Orange were commodious motel-like singles for all, married couples included. This time our comfortable beds were made up and ready for us, but as it turned out, we wouldn't have nearly enough opportunity to use them. We rushed to unpack, rushed to report for dinner, and continued rushing all that week; frantic, busy, happy, certainly stimulated, and learning, learning, learning.

Classes at Orange included land use, forestry management and other environmental topics, as well as the geology and minerals of New South Wales. Some of us were now learning to sleep with our eyes open. But everyone was in attendance and fully awake for the classes on wool production. Sitting in the shearing shed, with dozens of prize sheep mournfully gazing at us from crowded holding pens, we learned about intense-selection breeding—an ongoing project that tracks genetic characteristics of sheep by computer in an effort to propagate certain desirable traits. We had a try at shearing the raw wool; the complexities of dying wool using nature's products (lichen, mushrooms, flowers, roots) were outlined.

For a few stalwarts, Felix held a prebreakfast exercise class. Word of our puny efforts immediately spread and the nearby trees became laden with onlookers—kookaburra birds, who vented their loud and raucous mirth at our every creaky bend. Our stay at Orange was capped for me by the ride back to campus in my dinner hosts' car as a kangaroo hopped and vaulted in front of us for two miles. Then there was our outing to a vast 3,500-acre agricultural spread where the dashing owner inadvertently let drop his unmarried status, setting off a sort of behavioral gavotte that I blush to remember.

We left the hospitable citizens of Orange with fond and tearful farewells, our luggage now bearing personalized scrolls proclaiming each of us an honorary citizen of Australia's Big Apple, as Orange proudly bills itself. Our next destination was the Bawley Point Field School of Woolongong University. . . .

At Bawley Point, a trek to the toilets (at one end of the vast park) became a public event, as did a meander to the 20-cent showers (at the opposite end). At all times, of course, we had to be careful about scorpions hiding in corners, on toilet seats, in our shoes. Not to mention the snakes.

However compelling the classes on the local flora and fauna, forest management, soil erosion, the wetlands and local mammals, one look at the unbelievable beach right over the hill and I too was over the hill whenever possible, to the endless expanse of white sand rimming the sparkling aqua Tasman Sea.

At Bawley Point we learned how to catch possums and marsupial mice in cages with trap doors (after we studied them, we let them go unharmed); we had the opportunity to go on various field trips and spent a soggy, maniacal evening wandering through a rain forest. A few participants appeared to be disintegrating; others flourished.

At the week's end we returned to the now-beloved Sheraton Wentworth in Sydney for a two-day reunion with the other groups. There was a general dash for the bath and a sinking into of the bed, but civilization now seemed tame, with the sort of hazards we were all used to. We compared notes with other groups; rivalries developed as each band of pilgrims extolled the virtues of their own experiences and travels. A few budding romances were spotted, but in truth, most of our hearts now belonged to Australia, a country that had been opened to us in a unique fashion.

Finally, an article not by an Elderhostel participant, but by the son of a hosteling couple.*

## TRUST YOUR PARENTS

*by Tom Morain*

My parents are going to college. Under a program called Elderhostel, Iowa colleges and universities are offering one-week opportunities for Iowa senior citizens to take some special courses during the summer

---

*This article appeared on the editorial page of the *Jefferson Bee*, Jefferson, Iowa, and was subsequently reprinted in the first issue of *Between Classes*, vol. 1, no. 1, 1983, 3.

session. The week-long classes vary from campus to campus but cover a wide variety of topics: the future of democratic institutions, how to do your own genealogy, alternative energy sources for the future, ceramics, music appreciation, Iowa's Old Order Amish.

Students will sleep in the dormitories, eat in the food service cafeterias, and use the recreational facilities of the college. Mom and Dad are at Luther College in Decorah.

The Elderhostel program is great, but I'm a little anxious nevertheless. I've never had "college-kid" parents before, and while some of our concerns are silly, we can't help worrying about them anyway.

Should we let them have a car for the week they are there or will it interfere with their studies?

If they send their laundry home in the middle of the week, should we wash it and send it back or teach them that they have to learn to be responsible for their own things?

All the Elderhostel students will be in the same co-ed dorm for the week. Need we remind them of the dangers of proximity or do we rely on the example we have set at home? Is there anything we could tell them now that would help?

How often should we accept collect calls home? Of course we want to hear from them, but would it be rude to send a roll of stamps if they call too often?

If Mom takes up electric guitar and Dad brings home a set of drums, must we endure their practice sessions in the house? Do we have to listen to acid Welk?

If they seem to have more spending money than we think they went to school with, do we ask them where they are getting it? After all, it's hard to think of Mother as a pusher, but how are children to know these days?

Should we insist that the college send home their grades at midweek?

Would they be embarrassed if we visited them and asked to meet their friends?

How do you suggest to them nicely that just because they are going to college, they don't have to dress like bums? What if Mom wants to wear jeans to church next Sunday? What if Dad insists on fringing his ties? What, heaven forbid, if they start popping their gum when they talk?

Probably we're worrying needlessly. Most parents who go to college are clean, responsible and wholesome people who will be credits to their children and communities. But being a son or daughter in a rapidly changing world is a rough assignment. We want the most for our parents, but realize that we can't give them everything. We shall continue to love them—and hope for the best.

# CHAPTER ELEVEN

# TEACHING FOLKS
# WHO SIMPLY
# WANT TO KNOW

The story of Elderhostel is primarily the story of older citizens who are reaching out to new experiences, acting on their still-powerful interest in learning, and enjoying the challenge of new friendships with peers. Obviously, Elderhostel would not have been such a resounding success without them. But the elders represent only part of the story. In 1990 there were over 1,500 institutions enrolling more than 200,000 participant-weeks in programs year-round. For each of these programs there were teachers who, for a modest honorarium, introduced hostelers to a new world of ideas. And behind the scenes of all these flourishing programs there were forty-six state directors, along with six provincial directors in Canada. Without the hard work and dedication of these committed teachers and administrators, Elderhostel could not exist.

Many teachers, for whom the constant engagement with a college-age population has become tiring, discover the renewal that comes from a radically different set of learners. Elderhostel instructors do not have to field questions about "what will be on the test," nor face the blank stares of students more interested in jobs or graduate school than the subject at hand. Instead they find that their enthusiasm for teaching is rekindled by the refreshing and often spontaneous questions for which Elderhostelers are so well known. One Elderhostel teacher observed, "It is a wonderful thing to be involved in teaching folks who simply want to know."

What follows are the reflections of a few of the teachers, program directors, campus coordinators, and university administrators whose committed participation is so crucial to Elderhostel's success. Although each of the thousands of Elderhostel organizers across the country would likely have stories enough to fill a book, these few have been selected as a representative sample. Their testimonies convey the sense of rejuvenation that is gained by exposure to Elderhostelers.

### *Jill Bigler, Campus Coordinator, Mercer University*

Crying makes a bad impression on a new boss. But that's about what I was ready to do, reporting to my dean. I had just inspected the vacant residence hall that had to be ready in six weeks to receive its first-ever Elderhostel group.

"There is *nothing*," I mourned. "No shower curtains, no wastebaskets, no reading lights; *forget* light bulbs!"

So began my career in 1986 as Elderhostel coordinator for Mercer University, a midsized, coeducational institution in Macon, Georgia. Mercer had recently merged with a small women's college twenty-five miles from the main campus that, in its final year of existence, would temporarily house our Elderhostel programs. Fortunately, we had already lined up an excellent faculty, but the housing facilities were in an antiquated dormitory building, which had only squeaky student cots, utilitarian desks and chairs. And I had no budget for more (or better).

I quickly learned my first Elderhostel lesson: improvisation. For six weeks, while indulging in some truly creative deficit financing, I labored to bring the premises up to par. By the time the first thirty-six expectant participants arrived on campus, the building was more or less ready. (I learned about "less" later.)

The first two groups came and went uneventfully, accepting our still spartan southern hospitality gracefully, having a lot of fun in the process. I began to relax.

The "less" kicked in when the dorm's rustiest water pipe burst. Mopping frantically late one Sunday afternoon alongside two maintenance workers who definitely did not share my sense of urgency about reducing the flood in the bedrooms, I learned coordinator lesson number two: *never* be complacent.

A second experience was needed, however, for that lesson to take. As the year progressed without any more serious incidents, I began to dream of one last, memorable event for the final group before the campus closed. Because one of the college's best features was an Olympic-size, indoor swimming pool, a Hawaiian-born coworker and I conceived a combination student-Elderhostel luau featuring a suckling pig and hundreds of miniature tropical orchids. We would cast the orchids onto the pool's surface; students and Elderhostelers alike could dive for them. What a grand finale for the host campus!

The day of the big party I made a final inspection tour of the surroundings, now transformed into an ersatz Waikiki Beach. Food Services had outdone themselves: the serving table had a beautiful display of flowers and the pig sported a pineapple in its mouth. The orchids floated gently on the pool's surface; beach music wafted softly over the sound system. The pool's water temperature seemed a trifle cool, however, so I enjoined the maintenance man to turn up its thermostat a few degrees. Because neither he nor I was familiar with the pool building's relative temperature and humidity requirements, this was a big mistake.

Just after the Elderhostelers and students arrived, adorned in grass skirts, leis, festive shirts, and other tropical sportswear, it started to rain . . . inside the building! It rained and rained. The rising steam from the warming pool had collected on the ceiling and condensed. We had created a tropical rain forest! This turn of events caused considerable consternation among the Elderhostelers—the catalogue description which drew them to our campus said nothing about bringing rain gear for a party. (The students, more used to the anomalies of the pool, were slightly less surprised.)

Once we managed to discontinue the deluge and sponged off the pig, the party got back on track, enhanced by a multitude of wisecracks. One Elderhosteler even earned a large round of applause by leaping into the pool and rounding up the heat-wilted orchids, which he proudly presented to the female survivors of the near debacle.

Thus, my initial year ended with a splash, rather than a bang.

Knowing a year ahead of time that its Elderhostel "digs" would close, Mercer instituted a search for new program sites. Since its own residence halls remained full year-round, participants would have to be housed off the main campus—sometimes way off.

In 1987, we were asked by the Georgia state director to begin programming on coastal Georgia's Jekyll Island, 250 miles away from Mercer. The following year, we also initiated Elderhostels in Atlanta, seventy-five miles north of our Macon campus. From these arrangements arose coordinator lesson number three: keep your gas tank filled.

This was indelibly imprinted during Hurricane Hugo. Two days before Hugo inundated South Carolina, my current Jekyll Island Elderhostel group and I wore a steady path into the carpet of the cocktail lounge in the motel where the program was held—not so much in pursuit of a between-class nip as of weather updates on the wide screen television. The hurricane's eye filled the screen, bearing down on our tiny corner of the state. All night long the sound of hammers pounding plywood over the vast oceanfront expanses of plate glass served to underscore our collective concern. The next day, we discussed evacuation procedures.

On Thursday, the Georgia State Patrol ordered all tourists to vacate the island—at once! According to plan, forty-eight of fifty Elderhostelers took to their cars and departed across the causeway to the mainland, scattering west, south, and north. Left behind were two sisters-in-law who had come by bus up Florida's east coast and could not return because bus service was temporarily suspended. And me.

The three of us quickly loaded all our belongings into my car and, gas tank full, we too, hastened to higher ground. For the better part of a day we explored the tiny towns of south Georgia, hoping to find a bus stop that still featured buses. We finally found one in an inland city, where my fellow travelers got the last motel room in town, with a king-size bed. I left them there, engrossed in a debate as to how their incompatible body climate controls would adapt to the one-bed situation.

Those two were more fortunate than our other evacuees who headed northeast along the coast. Though it missed Jekyll Island completely, the northward-veering hurricane caught up with some as they stopped for the night in the Charleston-Myrtle Beach areas.

The following week we mailed participants graduation certificates proclaiming them "Hugo Hostelers," and granting them special dispensation to share personal escapades with subsequent Elderhostel compatriots.

Like the Florida sisters, who viewed the evacuation as an adventure, most of our Elderhostelers over the past five years have been great sports and delightful people. Equipped with a zillion life experiences and often zany senses of humor, they provide zest to academia's jaded practitioners. Their arrival each Sunday is the highlight of a coordinator's job, which is otherwise dogged by the nemesis of paperwork.

Processing fifty people a week, every week, plus working with 150 instructors requires megareams of paper and megahours of preparation. My worst nightmare as a coordinator is that I might expire on a Tuesday with *all those people* due the next Sunday, the paperwork left unfinished. Or, far worse, that my assistant might expire instead.

After making arrangements for instruction, foresight and the management of endless details are the essence of the campus coordinator's role in the grand scheme of Elderhostel. Not to mention being available at all times.

Although the coordinator sees hundreds of faces, each Elderhosteler is unique: occasionally predictable, always fascinating. Some first-timers almost tiptoe into registration, their body language betraying hidden apprehensions at the prospect of having to live, study, eat, and interact for *five whole days* with more than forty strangers. Such shyness usually evaporates by orientation when the "veterans" inevitably enfold them with warmth and laughter. New widows and other singles, sometimes timid about venturing far from home bases alone, likewise are embraced and supported. Recent retirees from very disciplined fields—science, engineering, the military—occasionally find it difficult to adapt to the easygoing, communal atmosphere, which represents such a departure from the rigid routines of their previous workaday worlds. But whatever their backgrounds, by week's end everyone is happily joined in the common causes of learning new things and experiencing that wonderful interpersonal communication so typical of Elderhostelers.

Because my own position has slowly evolved from a "one-woman show" campus coordinator to that of an administrator overseeing seventeen part-time, on-site coordinators, I miss the daily contact with the Elderhostelers. I must now leave the give and take, the jokes, the personal side of the program to other individuals. To them I bequeath the pleasure of hearing a former concert pianist's brilliant performance on a piano ordinarily pounded by local rock groups in our motel's lounge. The on-site personnel are the ones lucky enough to be regaled with accounts of sled dog racing by a retired network executive, or the travels of a former publisher who once carried the Hope diamond in his pocket on the New York City subway. Although they must be the first to deal with the inevitable complaints, how satisfied they must be when problems are resolved on the spot. If not, they'll find me. Day or night.

I continue to coordinate a few programs on-site each year—enough to "keep me humble," as my state director is fond of saying—but the most memorable times were those novitiate years, when the water pipe burst or when a dorm fire forced 150 female students to move in with the Elderhostelers, causing carefully segregated bathrooms to become coeducational overnight.

Elderhostel policies preclude tipping the coordinator. However, I once received an after-the-fact thank you that certainly matched the occasion. Mercer's policy forbidding students to drink on campus extends to all guests. Early in the week of one on-campus program I noticed that a very personable gentleman, fully aware of this policy, still visited his room more often than even a serious physiological malfunction might warrant. Each time he returned to class or elsewhere, his joviality seemed elevated by several degrees. Eventually I encountered him during an evening stroll across campus, cocktail glass held high. After pausing to talk, I hugged him, then said, "Joe, you're either going to have to go on the wagon this minute for the rest of the week or else sashay down the street to the Holiday Inn lounge in your off hours." A nice guy to the core, he became very apologetic and hustled back to his room. For the rest of the week he was an exemplary student. At program's end, when I opened my car door to load equipment, I found a note on the driver's seat: "Thanks. Joe." Alongside the note was a bottle of Jack Daniels.

I also recall Betty and Bob. An ardent golfer, Bob played several times during a Jekyll Island program. His third round was interrupted by a nasty heart attack, which ultimately required quadruple bypass surgery in the nearest major city, Jacksonville. I helped Betty rearrange her life and plans for the rest of the Elderhostel week as she moved to the local hospital where Bob underwent final tests and preoperative preparations. After my return to Macon, an on-site coordinator and I followed Bob's progress by telephone until he was safely repaired and back home. During one conversation he stated, "We'll be back next year."

A year later, as promised, there they were—at the fringes of a registration crowd, waving to attract my attention. After preliminary hugs and exchanges Bob said, "Well, we just wanted to say hello. We're attending the (another college—a competitor) Elderhostel program up the road."

Elderhostel does indeed keep one humble.

Elderhostelers' approach to life and learning buoys the campus coordinator. Those of us nearing retirement age find that, by using them as models, we have much more to look forward to as retirees than we imagined. Our dedicated faculty are likewise energized, sometimes rising from sickbeds to keep their commitments to the program.

For them, and for hundreds of other coordinators like me, the reward is knowing these people: fine, friendly people who are singularly enthusiastic. So enthusiastic are they that I smile even now while writing one final anecdote. It sums up pretty well the frustrations, the joys, and the humor which pervade the work of a campus coordinator.

Chasing after one group (later dubbed "the most prompt group in Mercer's history"), I tried to wiggle through their ranks as they marched determinedly from the school bus toward their first class of the week. Realizing I would never make it to the front where I could shepherd them along the maze of campus sidewalks, I summoned my best vocal projection powers and yelled, "Wait for *me*! *I'm* supposed to be your leader."

They just kept going. And I hope Elderhostel always will.

## *Marilyn Couture, Teacher, Linfield College**

The opportunity to teach Elderhostel was first presented to me in 1980 when I was an adjunct professor of anthropology at Linfield College in McMinnville, Oregon. I was coleading natural history tours with botanist Lucile Housley and studying Native American ethnobotany, and it was always a pleasure to share these interests with students. So, innocently enough, we accepted the invitation. I had no idea how much my life would be touched by Elderhostelers for the next decade.

Most Elderhostel universities offer traditional classes on campus, but we wanted to focus our program on field-oriented courses. Our non-traditional learning forays took us to Malheur Field Station in southeastern Oregon, which seemed the perfect location to study cultural and natural history. The students enjoyed the field trips; the only real complaint was that the doggone school bus didn't have enough leg room. We managed to deal with the bumpy ride by adding pillows and using a damp towel to seal off the dust that leaked through the door. We also figured that if we filled the hostelers with enough knowledge of the area and delicious food, they might overlook the discomforts and enjoy the class.

Enjoy it they did, and their recommendations brought us many more

*Couture was active in Linfield's Elderhostel program from 1980 to 1988. Though still teaching regular credit courses at Linfield, she now leads Elderhostel programs at other centers for learning in Oregon.

students. As the demand for classes grew, Linfield responded by expanding the program. We took trips to Cannon Beach and Columbia Gorge, a world-class natural feature. Students, in turn, responded by returning to the programs and demanding a more vigorous experience. Lucile and I developed a two-week intensive class entitled "The Ocean, The Mountains, The River, and The Desert: Environmental Concerns."

In 1984 and 1985 we transported forty Elderhostelers and their gear 1,700 miles in a yellow school bus to study the ecology of Oregon. Students traipsed with us over the countryside to smell wild flowers, key them out; sample an array of wild edibles; look at Indian rock art, ancient rock shelters, and prehistoric tools. We learned about the environment element by element, taking things down to their core.

The hostelers found the natural history fascinating, but were equally interested in issues they could relate to more directly. Lively discussions ensued over balancing economics with preservation: what to do about old growth forests and the spotted owl, threatened salmon, preservation of the Columbia Gorge, and the impact of grazing on public lands. They were concerned with how their tax dollars were being spent by the federal government.

A primary concern was trying to present both sides of these issues and being candid about our own biases, though it was hard not to take sides at times. Elderhostelers generally have the time and inclination to write letters of support or criticism on public issues, and it would be nice to have them on "our" side. Believe me, their letters make a difference.

From over a decade of Elderhostel memories, two experiences stand out.

*Something for everyone.* Obviously "drug along" by his wife, one man sat at the back of the bus with his eyes closed and his transistor radio attached to his ear, tuned to baseball for nearly the entire session. I happened to overhear him comment to another participant that he would like to see a rattlesnake. So on the last day I altered our itinerary and plotted our trip to pass along a well-known rattler den I had been

Bravo! Hostelers applaud their lecturer during an Elderhostel session at the Blooms-burg University of Pennsylvania.

avoiding for years. As I announced the feature to the group and cautioned everyone to exercise care, the man leapt out of his seat, raced up the aisle of the bus, and scrambled up the rimrock. With a loud acclaim he spotted a big rattler coiled and wedged in a crevice between two rocky faces. Once aboard the bus he proclaimed that this was the best Elderhostel he had ever attended.

*The party animal.*    A semiretired florist carried fresh yellow roses 350 miles across the desert to the wine and cheese social hour the first evening of our program. He announced: "If you would like to see this continue each afternoon, fill my hat and I'll take care of the rest." We were thirty-five miles from the nearest store, but that didn't deter him. He found every excuse to get us to drive the school bus to Frenchglen general store. When that didn't work, he drove the thirty-five miles himself to purchase libations. Needless to say, it was a very relaxed session.

Elderhostel works so well because it provides a structured, nontraditional learning experience that fills a societal niche. The programs are presented in a pleasurable environment by skilled instructors, which allows people with common interests to express themselves. In contrast to "traditional"-age college students, there is very little posturing among Elderhostel participants. These students are secure in the fact that they know who they are and how they came to be.

It is for very selfish reasons that I continue to teach Elderhostel programs. I have learned a great deal from the participants, who represent all walks of life. I witnessed the thrill a retired forester experienced when he saw himself in an archaeological film I presented. The archival footage from 1935 showed him as a student excavating a site with Professor Luther Cressman. I get a great deal of personal satisfaction from sharing and expanding knowledge.

Beyond that, I count my blessings for the number of Elderhostel friends I have made. I have visited them on trips through the United States, stayed with their relatives when I've travelled overseas, and I count many former "students" among my very best friends.

"The joy of Elderhostel doesn't end with Saturday morning!"

*Jay E. Fields, Teacher, Missouri Southern State College*\*

I didn't even know what "an elderhostel" was. I had stayed in youth hostels in Europe, so when someone asked me if I wanted to be involved with an Elderhostel program hosted by the university where I was teaching, I honestly believed I would be part of a construction team, building fixed-income housing for the senior citizens in our com-

---

\*Excerpted and adapted from "A First-Person 'Hands-On' Experience in Innovative Higher Education . . . Elderhostel: A Multidisciplinary Approach (An Instructor's Viewpoint)," published in the journal *Innovative Higher Education*, Spring/Summer 1986. The experiences chronicled here occurred when Dr. Fields was teaching in Kentucky. At the time of writing, however, Fields was an associate professor of dramatic arts at San Diego State University; he has since moved to Missouri Southern State.

munity. Perhaps that work would have been easier! I had no idea what I was getting myself into.

It all began when Dot, a physical education instructor at the university, and a senior citizen and grandmother herself, dropped by my office to discuss her proposal for an Elderhostel experience on our campus. I had no knowledge of the program, but Dot explained that our guests would come from all over the country, selecting our area primarily for the beauty and historical interests of the location (near Lexington, Kentucky), and that we had to offer three classes. In most cases, Dot continued, the classes were not related in content. She showed me an example offered by another university: "The Dead Sea Scrolls," "Journal Writing," and "Computer Software." This was the part that Dot didn't like. Her proposal was a "multidisciplinary approach" in which the three instructors would work closely together, attend each others' classes, and structure sessions as outgrowths and extensions of their colleagues' classes. Where most teachers in Elderhostel programs were required to teach one class session per day, Dot wanted us, in addition to teaching our specialized class, to attend two other sessions per day and to integrate our offerings. And she asked for two more things: complete dedication to the project and *lots of energy.*

I had never met Dot before that day, but she had heard that my work in the drama department was marked by a high energy level and constant drive, and she wanted those qualities in her partners for the team-teaching project she proposed. Our third cohort was Art, a music professor, who had taught many workshops in music "therapy" as well as writing several articles on the subject. Dot's plan was to offer three courses (physical education, music, and drama) under one "umbrella," calling it "Languages of Creativity." Our ultimate goal for the week would be to incorporate all the activities and learning experiences from the three classes into a final unified program that the Elderhostelers would perform. This creative event would be videotaped and given to all performers as a remembrance of their week together.

As the three of us discussed these ideas with the university Elderhostel office, we unanimously agreed that we wanted to spend as much time with the senior students as possible—to get to know them outside the classroom. We were invited to stay in the dorms with them, even to bring our families along, the belief being that they might enjoy our children. We decided to eat all of our meals with them, to personally transport them in the university vans from class to class, and to chauffeur them to the various outside events during the week (the Kentucky Horse Park in Lexington; a Shaker Village in Pleasant Hill, Kentucky; a wine and cheese party at a nearby country home; and an old-fashioned Kentucky dinner, complete with spoon bread, at a small diner on the Kentucky River). In short, we planned to "become" Elderhostelers for that week. As it turned out, we spent more time with them outside of class than in, which really became the most exciting part of my first experience with Elderhostel. In fact, as I think back to that week, if one were to ask me what I did, I would probably respond, "I drove around Kentucky with an Elderhostel group—oh yes, I also taught them a drama class."

. . . Monday morning, our first full day, began with Dot's exercise class at 7 A.M. In our most stylish running outfits and gym shorts, we stretched and grunted (Art and I groaned louder than the Elderhostelers, Dot didn't even perspire), and jogged around the lobby of the dormitory in grand style. The only complaint they had about Dot's program was that they also wanted to go swimming before breakfast; an early morning swim became part of the exercise class the very next day. After breakfast came Art's music class, where in the first session, they were composing melodies and lyrics on a variety of instruments Art had provided.

The first drama class became a brainstorming session to establish a universal theme to which all could relate while permitting everyone to bring something individual and personal to the script. After much discussion, we arrived at a title, "Memorable Moments of Meaning," which would permit everyone to recall specific events from his/her life that could be shared with the group. These "remembrances," along with physical activities and musical interludes, would become our play, and we chose to present it in readers' theatre fashion—the performers being permitted to carry scripts from which they "interpreted" their various stories.

The first day set the schedule and tempo for the week: exercises, breakfast, music class, lunch, drama class, extracurricular activity, dinner, and, if needed, more rehearsal time. Each morning, as Dot led the group through various physical warm-ups, everyone searched for specific movements which might be used in the "play." Art waited for a finished script (hah!) around which he would add the music. I taped each of their memorable moments on a cassette recorder, and from the two-and-a-half hours of material, compiled a forty-minute script (before music and movement were added). Next I typed and distributed the scripts, blocked the show, and located the needed props, while Art procured the musical instruments. The Elderhostel office arranged for the banquet and the taping. By Thursday, things were getting a bit hectic; opening (and closing) night was one day away. That afternoon, in the midst of our "theatrical activities," while driving the "actors" from class to class to rehearsals to meals (in two different vans, both of which I was driving), arranging a trip to Shakertown for later that day, and babysitting my daughter (she tagged along to nearly all the events), I lost the keys to my own car, the tape recorders with the scripted tapes, AND ONE OF THE VANS! It took over an hour to find the van (I simply could not remember where I had parked it), the recorder was at home, and my keys did not show up for several days. The day reached a climax when, driving back to campus from Shakertown along a lovely back road (I had decided to avoid the Interstate and show our out-of-state visitors the beauty of Kentucky), the narrow highway suddenly dead-ended—INTO THE KENTUCKY RIVER. Just when I thought I would probably have to turn around and retrace every mile to return by the Interstate, we noticed a very small barge chugging slowly to our bank. Sure enough, it was a ferry boat, and for $2.00, the man would take us across to the other bank. What a thrill for me! I had lived in that area for four years, had heard that the ferry boat still existed, but had never been able to locate it. Now I felt like an expert tour guide—adding a little local color to the Elderhostelers' stay in the bluegrass state.

No matter how enjoyable these outings were, my mind was always on the production we had to stage in twenty-four hours. Rehearsals continued, music was still being written, and Dot and I began to combine our classes, attempting to juxtapose movement and literature so they complemented each other. The creative process continued until Friday morning; the performance was that night.

Dignitaries of the university, Elderhostel staff workers, and instructors' friends and families were invited to the banquet and performance. After a formal catered dinner, cameras were readied, and the cast was called to places. For the opening number, the ensemble accompanied themselves on dulcimers, cymbals, and a drum while singing the following lyrics to the tune of "As the Saints Go Marching In":

> We've been creating the whole week long,
> And now we're going to give a show.
> We hope that you will like it,
> But if not, don't let us know!

The script had been divided into three sections: childhood days, growing older, and the future. After the song, the narrator began: "First of all, we thought about our childhood days. I grew up in . . ." at which point each cast member announced his/her home city and state. Then selected stories/remembrances were shared (generally accompanied by some background music which was appropriate to the subject matter of the story). During this childhood section, the performers shared their memories directly with the audience, recreating images and emotions just as they had occurred the first time, many years ago. At one point, using beach balls and scarves, each person simultaneously "danced" interpretive moves, recreating some special event of their youth. It was truly a lovely moment in the production.

Next the group moved into the growing older section, where, accompanied by "I'm Forever Blowing Bubbles," each one shared feelings about their present lives:

I think growing older is wonderful. Now that I'm retired, I've been having the best time of my life, doing what I want to do when I want to do it.

You know, you really don't have the time to do all the things you thought you would do. I started to carve a life-sized figure out of a 30" tree, and I found that there was so much wood on the outside, I was having a hard time getting into the part that I wanted to carve.

I think the hardest part about growing older is losing so many people you love. Now you have time to do all these wonderful things, you wish you had more friends to share things with.

I'm having trouble with it, and that's all I want to say about that.

When you get older, you realize that you're the older generation, and you have no one to go to. You're it!

The only thing wrong with old age is that it doesn't last long enough.

And finally after each one made a comment, a lady stepped forward from behind the rest of the performers and shouted: "Hold it! I have a problem with all this attention on memory . . . looking to the past. I really think it's a crock. We ought to call this "new perspectives." I'll be darned if I want to think about what *was*. I want to think about what *is* and what *will be*."

At this point, the script moved into the future, and someone said, "Let's think about the future, what we'd like to do." The following lines were among those offered during this section of the play:

Expectations, fantasies! I have a fantasy of being somebody's mistress. I also want to be a famous dancer.

I have a fantasy of playing Willy Loman in *Death of A Salesman* and Grandfather in *You Can't Take it With You.*

Of spending a winter in Italy.

Of being rich as Onassis.

Of finishing that carving out of that 30" tree.

Of raising an orchid that would carry my name.

I'd like to learn to fly a plane. I can't even use a screwdriver.

I want to be one of the first women into space. I even have a letter composed, telling them that my training has all been in the direction of observing, and routine doesn't bother me, and I don't take up much room. It's time they had more women up there.

After each person had a chance to voice his/her future hopes, Art underscored on the piano as one member from the cast stepped forward and delivered the famous lines from *Man of La Mancha*, "To dream the impossible dream." Then they all formed a straight line across the front of the stage, each taking the hand of the person next to him/her until they had all linked themselves together in friendship, and sang a final song: "Growing old is such fun; we recommend it for everyone."

To complete the evening, we all gathered around a large television screen and viewed a playback of the evening's performance. It was quite an exciting way to end our week of creativity.

Saturday morning I felt I had one more task to perform: meet each Elderhosteler in the dormitory lobby and help carry luggage to his or her car and bid each one a "good trip home." What a wonderful experience the week had been! I felt a warm fondness for this group of people with whom I had shared nearly every second during that week, and for some reason I really felt good about myself. I know that Dot's multidisciplinary approach, combined with our decision to become part of the group were the main reasons I felt so positive about the experience.

Several years later I was involved with another Elderhostel program in San Diego, California. We did not select the combined classes technique, but it was still a uniquely exciting experience. I must close with a little anecdote because I feel it sums up perfectly the attitudes of these marvelous senior citizens who are so young in spirit. One lady, in her late sixties, wanted to go to the San Diego Zoo. My only transportation was my motorcycle. No matter. She put on my leather jacket, my helmet, and clinging tightly to my waist, flew along the California freeways, constantly talking in my ear about what a wonderful experience her first Elderhostel week was turning out to be.

*George E. Arquitt, State Director, Oklahoma State University*

It was the summer of 1975, and I was standing with two colleagues in the lobby of an Oklahoma State University residence hall, greeting participants in "Project Intergenerational Living." The Project was a summer program designed to study the interaction between college students and older adults. As each of the twenty older adults arrived, it became clear that there was a real adventure in store for us all. Already we began to realize what the rest of the summer's experience would demonstrate: age differences do not impede human relationships, but foster them.

Unbeknownst to those of us in Oklahoma, during this same summer Elderhostel was being born at the University of New Hampshire. It wasn't until the 1979 meetings of the Association for Gerontology in Higher Education, at which I presented the results of our 1975 project, that I became fully aware of that other educational venture for older adults. At the association meetings I met Elderhostel's state director for Iowa, Peggy Houston, who told me about the organization and introduced me to its national representatives.

At the time I had no inkling that the program she described would become a focal point for my life and work. However, several months later I received a call from Boston asking me to consider organizing an Elderhostel program in Oklahoma. After some thought I agreed, and I have been hooked ever since.

From the start, Elderhostel has been a constant challenge to my organizational skills and entrepreneurial spirit. Two weeks before the first-ever Oklahoma Elderhostel began, there were only six people enrolled on our campus. But I was determined to have a program. I beat the local bushes and was able in the two remaining weeks to round up nine locals who would participate as commuters. Fifteen provided a critical mass for a successful program, and what a week we had! Every one of us had been bitten by the "Elderhostel bug."

The next year we grew to three colleges and one of the weeks at OSU was attended by over forty Elderhostelers. Each year more schools and sites were added; now we can claim eighteen. Somewhere along the way, directing Oklahoma's Elderhostel stopped being a "moonlight" to my job as professor of sociology, and was identified as an official part of my work load at the university.

The role of state director is multifaceted. The director must keep

Elderhostelers in a drawing class at the Minneapolis College of Art and Design. (Photo by Rik Sferra)

tabs on existing Elderhostel programs, making sure that they are of the highest possible quality in terms of academics, facilities, and coordinators. Host institutions are encouraged to expand their offerings, and the state director guides the development of new courses. A director must also be continually on the lookout for new and creative opportunities for program development across the state. Finally, the director promotes Elderhostel throughout the state, spreading the word to all eligible participants and institutions.

Through my statewide travels and personal contacts as Elderhostel state director I have been introduced to many parts of Oklahoma that I hadn't seen before, including its numerous colleges and universities, and a great variety of geographical, environmental, and cultural gems. It has been a joy, in turn, to introduce Oklahoma to Elderhostel participants, many of whom tell me that their perceptions of the state change very much for the better after their Elderhostel experiences. I am convinced that Elderhostel is good for the state as a whole.

As Elderhostel has grown in Oklahoma, and along with it my responsibilities, I have found it increasingly difficult to balance the roles of state director and campus coordinator with the roles of teacher, researcher, and advisor that are crucial to my position as a faculty member at OSU. Because I refuse to diminish commitment to either of my two loves, I have integrated the roles to a large extent. I have shifted my teaching and research toward social gerontology, with special focus on public perceptions of aging and the impact of social and physical environmental differences on the aging process. Elderhostel has significantly impacted my focus as a professor and has become the centerpiece of my professional development. And Elderhostel provides an opportunity for my university students to get involved with older adults who often become role models, providing advice about careers and other matters.

Furthermore, as Elderhostel coordinator I have had to make contact with administrators, service providers, and faculty from other departments—rather than limit engagement to just *my* corner of campus, the sociology department. Elderhostel has helped me develop administrative skills, which are valuable in my latest role as department chair.

Elderhostel has also had a significant impact on my personal development. It has given me the chance to get involved with my greater social and physical environment. As a result of the many Elderhostel programs I have coordinated, I now count hundreds of older adults across the country as part of my friendship network. These contacts have caused me to grow intellectually as well as socially. In short, Elderhostel has given me the same opportunities for expansion that it offers to participants.

Of particular importance to me has been the national network of other state and provincial directors and the Boston staff. These people have become part of my "extended family" because of our work together over the course of thirteen years to create a more perfect Elderhostel. As Elderhostel has grown beyond our combined imagination we have experienced both the agony and the ecstasy of growth and development. When the demands of the growing organization pushed us in the direction of a typical bureaucratic structure, the personal ties of the Elderhostel community took hold and helped us fight the tendency toward depersonalization. As a result, we have been able to maintain an organization that, though necessarily bureaucratic in some ways, is bureaucracy with a human face.

The national community of organizers not only provides opportunities for the exchange of new ideas, and a social setting to celebrate our successes, but also provides a support group to soothe the inevitable wounds of disappointment when things go wrong. Our deep commitment to maintaining the essentially personal nature of Elderhostel is what makes it unique among other national programs for older adults. I believe that the strong sense of community among the state directors and national staff trickles down, facilitating an equally strong sense of community among all who participate.

Elderhostel has been a boon to all who have experienced it: participants, campus coordinators, faculty, national staff, and state directors. It has developed far beyond what many of us anticipated during the early years, and will be expanding even more dramatically in the future. We have seen only the tip of the iceberg.

One statement made ten years ago about Elderhostel, which continues to stay with me, came from my then nine-year-old daughter as she helped me with an Elderhostel program: "Daddy, do you think they will have Elderhostel when I'm old enough to go?" My answer, then and even more surely now, was a strong, "Yes, Karen."

*Hoke L. Smith, President, Towson State University*

Elderhostel has provided me with rich insight into the durability and flexibility of the human spirit.

I first had contact with the organization over a decade ago at Drake University, and I was immediately impressed by the participants and their enthusiasm for life. I also know of Elderhostel's importance and impact more personally—my mother has participated in several programs. For her, the opportunity for travel and friendship afforded by Elderhostel has been a source of rejuvenation and continuing exploration.

When I became President of Towson State University, in Towson, Maryland, I encouraged our College of Continuing Education to develop an Elderhostel program. They did so and by all accounts the program has been a success. The presence of Elderhostelers on the Towson campus has been both a delight and an inspiration. During the summer months the University hosts a number of programs, including day camps for young children. To witness Elderhostel participants in their seventies, eighties, and nineties eating in the cafeteria alongside campers who are seven or eight truly shows that learning is for individuals of all ages.

Of the many Elderhostel participants who have visited Towson State, several individuals stand out in my memory. One was an eighty-two-year-old retired nun from Washington, D.C., who exercised every morning at 7:00, bounding up four flights of steps. Another, enrolled in a course on "The Golden Age of Radio," had been the chief sound effects technician for CBS for over thirty years, working with Jack Benny and other celebrities; the class discussion was enlivened considerably by his expert input. A similar situation occurred in a course on the military history of World War II, when the account of a crucial mission was corroborated by a class member who had actually flown that mission.

Many of the participants at Towson State's Elderhostel program are attracted by our proximity to Baltimore, and we take full advantage of the rich opportunities in the city. Last year we had a wine-and-cheese party and video nights; attended a Baltimore Symphony Summer Fest concert, an Inner Harbor trip (including three museum visits), Maryland Arts Festival offerings in drama, and a solar eclipse demonstration and lecture; visited an Asian Arts Gallery; and held a mixer with visiting students from London.

The most wonderful aspect of Elderhostel is that it benefits all involved—the "guests" as well as the "hosts." For the participants, it provides an opportunity for continuing intellectual and personal vitality. For the institution, it provides stimulation for the participating faculty and renewed commitment to the importance of lifelong learning.

Of course, we believe that the Towson State University Elderhostel is outstanding (and we have many comments to support this view), but what I hear from administrators at other host institutions indicates that the enriching success of our program is typical. Elderhostel is a vital part of the University.

# PART III

# The
# Theme

# CHAPTER TWELVE

# ELDERS IN AMERICA:
# THE CONTEXT FOR
# SUCCESS

The remarkable growth of Elderhostel has not taken place within a vacuum. In fact, the program's success directly correlates with the societal context of the period in which it has developed. To put it mildly, these have been revolutionary times for elders.

Approximately two-thirds of the men and women who have reached the age of sixty-five in all of human history are living today. Between 1960 and 1988 the number of Americans over sixty-five increased from 16,675,000 (9.2 percent of the population) to 30,367,000 (12.3 percent of the population), and it is estimated that between 1990 and the year 2000 the number of people over the age of seventy-five years will increase by 26.2 percent.

This dramatic growth in the number of older people has been matched by an equally dramatic rise in their quality of life. The poverty rate for Americans sixty-five years and older declined from 24.6 percent in 1970 to 12.2 percent in 1987; per capita discretionary income among the same group is now greater than for any other age category. In 1987 just over one-fourth of those sixty-five and older had a net income (per household) over $25,000.[1]

Furthermore, Federal programs currently provide an unprecedented degree of financial aid and regulatory support for older citizens. Approximately 30 percent of the Federal budget is expended annually in support of programs and benefits for the elderly. Clearly, the graying of the population has brought a great deal of political power to older Americans. This is understandable given the fact that there are now over

30,000,000 members of the American Association of Retired Persons (AARP).

An increasingly older population and its corresponding rise in spending power, educational level, and political power have made older people a more promising commercial market for retailers. Health delivery systems, pharmaceutical houses, travel agencies, car rental firms, restaurants, retirement communities, stock brokerage firms, insurance companies, and even colleges and universities are among those who have directed their advertising efforts to the senior citizen. Those at midlife (fifty years) and beyond have been characterized quite literally as "the $800 billion market."[2]

At the leading edge of the older population is a core of people who are "young-old, affluent-old, and educated-old"—an assertive middle-class constituency that is increasingly conscious of the options still available to them. These are the elders who are ready—physically, mentally, and financially—for new experiences.

The number of healthy elders with ample financial resources to meet their basic needs has created a vast market for programs that satisfy an additional one: the need for self-fulfillment. As we have moved beyond a deficient medical model for aging to one that stresses opportunities, rather than limits, millions of elders have rejected roles of disengagement and have opened themselves to new ideas. One Arizona Elderhosteler said, "Too many people have been sold a bill of goods about getting older. They think it's 'quitsville.' Nonsense! Go ahead and dream and do everything you can."

This post-materialistic motivational structure is perhaps most helpfully characterized by Maslow's term "self-actualization."[3] When people get older, many of them become more interested in learning for its own sake, as an end in itself, rather than as a means to an end. Knowledge and aesthetic interests rather than practical or material gain become motivations for activity. As the quantity of years remaining becomes realistically smaller, quality of life becomes a matter of increasing concern.

In his work dealing with consumer behavior, David Wolfe has divided adult life into three experiential stages: the *possession experi-*

A friendly bear hug for one hosteler on the campus of Prince William Sound Community College in Valdez, Alaska. (Photo by Edwin Morgan)

*ence stage* of young adulthood, the *catered experience stage* of the middle adult years, and the *being experience stage* that is seen as beginning in the sixth decade of life.[4] "Being experiences," those most characteristic of people sixty and over, are inner growth experiences with a substantially nonmaterialistic focus. Wolfe points out that in the late stages of life many adults find that the previously-idealized leisure lifestyle wears thin. Rejecting their fantasy of retirement as "time off," they search for new relationships, new activities, and new meaning in their lives. In *The Ulyssean Adult*, John McLeish has similarly demonstrated that many older adults embark on new careers in an attempt to fulfill their compelling personal needs.[5]

There are various ways of characterizing the changing interests and patterns of motivation that often come with the passage of years, but it is clear that many adults do launch themselves on new life adventures. They see their later years as a time to voyage again, to sail upon new waters, to continue a process of engagement in life.[*]

With the rise of the "young-old" population, the "scene [was] set for a much greater demand for education from older people than ever before. Not only are there more of them, probably in better health, but [they are aware] of retirement as a major stage in life, to be used and enjoyed."[6]

Between 1969 and 1981, the number of people sixty-five and older who participated in adult education almost tripled. By 1990, the National Center for Educational Statistics reported that almost 395,000 Americans fifty and over were enrolled in institutions of higher education.[7] R. J. Havighurst notes, there is a "significant correlation between the level of formal education achieved and participation in continuing education."[8] Since the American population is becoming more and more educated (between 1970 and 1988 the percentage of Americans with four or more years of college almost doubled, from 10.7 percent to 20.3 percent), it is likely that participation in adult education will continue to increase rapidly.[9]

---

[*] For an interesting and even inspirational account of personal renewal and commitment in the later years, see Jimmy and Rosalynn Carter's *Everything to Gain: Making the Most of the Rest of Your Life* (New York: Random House, 1987), p. 198 ff.

However, this growth in older learners is not necessarily reflected in increasing enrollments at traditional postsecondary institutions. Colleges and universities have long served adults through continuing education programs, but the focus of higher education has always been on younger collegiate and postcollegiate students. Though much is made of the isolated cases of older graduates at commencement time each year, they have been viewed as heartwarming exceptions—older persons who have succeeded in a young person's game.

But it has not been the exceptional graduating septuagenarian who has been changing things. For the most part, older adults have not been seeking enrollment in regular collegiate courses and programs because these programs are not suited to their needs or desires. As Harry R. Moody observes:

... the interests of older and younger adult learners are likely to be very different. Older learners tend not to be interested in credentials or degrees; they do not want tests, grades, or competition. On the contrary, they tend to be interested in participative learning that can promote immediate understanding or practical application. Older people cannot wait for a distant future.[10]

These differences are reflected in the terms *andragogy* and *pedagogy*. Andragogy, a concept popularized by Malcolm Knowles, is defined as "the art and science of helping adults learn," as opposed to pedagogy, which refers to the instruction of children.[11] Educational gerontologist Victor Agruso explains that "andragogy is based on assumptions that older learners are more concerned with solutions or approaches to immediate, rather than to long range, problems; they enter a learning experience with wide, diversified histories, thereby having a particular set to learn; and they are, in general, independent and self-directed."[12]

The pedagogical norm in colleges and universities is not suited to the andragogical needs of elders whose primary goal, as described by Maslow, is self-actualization. Teaching style, curricular design, and course content are most often focused on eighteen- to twenty-two-year-old students. Understandably, many older adults report that their educational needs are not met by conventional college courses.

In addition to these fundamental incompatibilities, there are a number of barriers to the involvement of elders in traditional college programs. Three main types of barriers have been identified:

1. Situational: elders may have difficulty finding transportation to campuses, or, if physically less able, getting around a sprawling campus once they are there.

2. Dispositional: elders may have negative self-images, such as perceiving themselves as "too old to learn," that make them apprehensive about mixing with younger students.

3. Institutional: high fees, inconvenient schedules, and other organizational structures may discourage elder participation.[13]

Whatever the reasons, it is clear that elders' needs cannot be met by traditional colleges and universities that have made no special efforts to accommodate a different learning population. Moody concludes, "This situation calls for much more innovation by institutions themselves, not just to respond to existing demand, but to create imaginative programs for a better educated aging population in the future."[14]

It is in the context of this need for innovation that Elderhostel was originally devised and continues to operate. From the beginning, Elderhostel has sought to provide learning opportunities designed *specifically* for elders. Although these programs often occur on college campuses, they are consciously different from the standard postsecondary fare.

The most obvious difference between Elderhostel courses and those at most colleges is, of course, the absence of required reading, homework, credits, or tests. Because it is assumed that Elderhostelers are motivated by love of learning, there is no need to assess formally their progress in mastering class materials. However, the courses are not mere fluff. Week-long courses are carefully screened for their academic content, and are designed to comprise a full seven and a half to ten contact hours of classroom or field experience.

There is something about the length of the programs that seems to be just right for most Elderhostel participants. Ten hours is enough time to receive a full introduction to a subject without being bogged down by highly specific details. The design of Elderhostel courses is not set in stone, however. When some hostelers expressed the desire to follow up in depth on certain subjects, for example, an Intensive Studies program was created. The length of the course remains the same—one week—but participants study only one subject, as opposed to three. In addition, participants *are* expected to do "homework" and a final paper or presentation is required.

The willingness to be flexible in order to meet the needs of its constituents sets Elderhostel apart from most educational organizations. The program also differs significantly from many other elder-oriented ventures, which are focused on travel and/or entertainment. Elderhostel's unique combination of leisure and learning is its trademark. Elderhostel seeks to maintain a balance between work and play, or, as the hosteler quoted in Chapter 1 put it, between "learning fun" and "fun fun." The residential format of the programs enhances both of these aspects, facilitating an atmosphere that is collegial in the truest sense of the word.

The most innovative feature of Elderhostel is surely the carefully-monitored curriculum. In their earliest conception of Elderhostel, Marty Knowlton and David Bianco were committed to programs that would be centered around liberal and humane studies. They resisted pressure to create or approve a curriculum that would be superficial, frivolous and, as Bianco likes to say, "all craftsy and done with bottles."

Equally important, they refused to allow the programs to feature topics having to do with aging. This policy resulted in one of Elderhostel's most distinctive features, and perhaps the greatest reason for its success—the paradox that it "offers age-segregated programming but with an explicitly 'age-irrelevant' curriculum."[15] Marty was afraid that teachers would not take elders seriously as students and would not give them challenging coursework; mandating that courses address liberal studies, rather than practical matters having to do with aging, was an attempt to counter this tendency.

There have been many times when proposals were made to offer Elderhostel courses on social security benefits, health care, wills and bequests, or Alzheimer's disease. These issues are certainly important to the over-sixty population, but the founders of Elderhostel believed that such topics would draw the participants' attention to illness and decline rather than competence, engagement, and, to borrow a term heard in conferences on aging, "functional wellness." It was Marty and David's view sixteen years ago, continually reaffirmed by Bill Berkeley and Mike Zoob today, that Elderhostel should focus on new powers that can be unleashed in the later years, rather than those which are lost with age.

By and large, this consciously age-irrelevant curriculum has accomplished just what its initiators hoped it would. Anybody who glances at the Elderhostel catalogue has no doubt that the courses are real and intellectually substantial. Moreover, hostelers appreciate the fact that, contrary to many elder-specific programs, Elderhostel courses are not condescending. One hosteler commented on this tendency: "You get sick and tired after a while of most senior citizens' programs. . . . They're always talking about your health or the problems of aging. But the mind is ageless." [16]

There are some, however, who argue that Elderhostel courses are not age-irrelevant. To the contrary, the lack of courses dealing specifically with elders' issues seems contrived, a head-in-the-sand avoidance of important topics. Increasingly there are those, including some members of the Elderhostel Board, who advocate that gerontological studies be offered, as long as they are organized and taught as liberal learning experiences.

There is a growing openness to this idea among the leadership of Elderhostel. Although courses on practical issues such as "How to get subsidized housing" or watered-down courses on "How to read to your grandchildren" will never be added to the Elderhostel curriculum, it is likely that courses examining the process of aging will begin to appear in some programs. There is already, for example, a course on the implications of hearing loss and impairment being offered at the Elderhostel program at Gallaudet University. This is appropriate, Bill Berkeley notes, because "we want institutions to do what they do best."

## ELDERHOSTELER DEMOGRAPHICS

In attempting to remain responsive to its particular clientele, Elderhostel must keep close tabs on just who participates in the programs. The demographics of Elderhostel participants have a profound effect on the way programs are planned and conducted.

Elderhostelers are by and large a self-selecting group of highly-motivated individuals. Mike Zoob says, "It's a demanding program, not like the commercial tours where they tell you what you'll be doing where, down to the last minute. Based on a seventy-five-word site description and a thirty-word program description, without knowledge about your roommate, you have to decide to go. Elderhostel definitely caters to risk-takers."

Moreover, these uncommonly venturesome individuals are not responding only to Elderhostel. A 1989 survey of participants in the United States and Canada revealed that 85.6 percent read AARP materials; 91.9 percent watch public television; 70.3 percent are involved in community service or volunteer work; 39.5 percent take academic courses as part of their regular activities; 23.0 percent own or regularly use a personal computer; and 20.2 percent participate in local politics.

Hostelers, then, are generally a rather privileged group. With important exceptions, they have had substantial prior education. In the same 1989 survey, 12.4 percent of participants reported an educational background of "high school or less"; 17.2 percent "some college"; 6.1 percent "two-year college associate"; 14.1 percent "four-year college graduate"; 18.1 percent "some postgraduate work"; 20.1 percent "masters degree"; 3.5 percent "Ph.D."; and 8.5 percent "law, medical, divinity, or other professional degree." To put it another way, over 80 percent of Elderhostelers have attended college, as opposed to 20 percent of the older population in America as a whole.[17]

There is, though, a small but significant portion of hostelers who have had relatively little formal education. In the early years of the program, the Elderhostel leadership worried about potential conflicts and

Elderhostelers practicing their strokes during a program at Strathcona Park Lodge, British Columbia. (Photo courtesy of Elderhostel Canada)

bad feelings that might arise if less-educated hostelers were in the same classroom as their highly-educated contemporaries. Their fears were allayed, however, by experiences such as one that Marty Knowlton remembers from the late 1970s:

A course was taught at the University of New Hampshire, a course on the Book of Job. Unbeknownst to the professor, in that course we had a retired editor of a Jewish journal of philosophy from London. We had the former chief rabbi of the Hebrew Theological Union. And we had a man who had been a judge at Nuremberg. When I told the professor . . . about these three people who were in her class she said, "Oh, which ones are they?"

In her classroom she also had a man who had graduated from high school only after he was sixty years of age, who had been a machinist all his life living in Brooklyn . . . and the professor couldn't decide which one that was either.

Obviously, this situation was extraordinary. But in the general course of Elderhostel programs, the differing educational backgrounds of participants rarely pose any problem.

Marty Knowlton originally intended that Elderhostel would benefit mostly low-income elders, but hostelers have always been primarily from the upper-middle class. Almost two-thirds of participants report an annual income of $30,000 or more.[18] Nonetheless, it has always been assumed by the Board and the administrative staff that Elderhostel should be made available to interested elders without regard to economic background. Consistent with this philosophy, a small percentage of each hosteler's tuition payment is put into a fund to provide scholarship support for those who might not otherwise be able to attend. Though the vast majority of Elderhostelers have no difficulty meeting program costs, these "hostelships" represent an important and enduring organizational commitment.

In conjunction with its commitment to economic diversity among participants, Elderhostel has also made an effort to reach out to minorities, but with relatively little success. The Boston office reports that fewer than 1 percent of participants are members of the major minority groups, a number which Bill Berkeley calls "pitifully small." The difficulty, as Berkeley sees it, is that "Elderhostel or any modest variation of it is not going to be appealing to those who haven't had firsthand experience with higher education. The vast majority of elders who have had such experiences are white and reasonably well off."

Even among black college graduates, however, Elderhostel does not fare well. Berkeley says that according to demographic studies Elderhostel should have about 3 percent black participation, but the organization has been "grossly underachieving in this group." Again, the problem is one of history and circumstance. "It's hard to tap into the network of educated blacks," Berkeley explains, "because those folks grew up in very segregated times. Somebody old enough to be in Elder-hostel today had already graduated from college by the time of *Brown* v. *Board of Education*."

In an attempt to remedy the situation, Elderhostel has stressed the development of programs at certain historically black colleges and at various urban institutions.[19] In addition, a minority recruitment staff member has been added at the national level. These initiatives offer promise of increased minority enrollment.

To round out the participant profile it should be noted that the majority of hostelers are single women. This is, in some sense, due to "pure demographics," as Bill Berkeley notes, because women live longer than men. The gender balance is less disproportionately female now than when the program was initiated, at which time most participants were women. In today's programs there are more men, as well as more couples.

The leaders of Elderhostel would like to reach a broader audience, but they see no need to apologize. "We are what we are," Berkeley says. "We're filling a need for the people we *do* serve. After all, retirement for anybody—even the middle class—can be very traumatic."

# CHAPTER THIRTEEN

# ELDERS TEACHING ELDERS: THE INSTI-TUTE MOVEMENT

As earlier chapters have shown, in just a decade and a half Elderhostel has become the leading educational venture for people of retirement age. It would be unfortunate and wrong, however, to suggest that Elderhostel was the only or the first initiative for elders to offer challenging opportunities for liberal arts learning. There have been other and earlier programs, many of which helped lay the groundwork for Elderhostel's success.

For many years, colleges and universities across the country have offered continuing education programs for their alumni and also for members of the local community. These programs have provided thousands of older Americans with the opportunity for entry, or reentry, into the academy—often at very low cost.

Beginning in the 1970s, many colleges experimented with innovative approaches to education specifically for seniors. Eckerd College in Florida built on-campus housing for elders to facilitate their continuing participation in educational programs.[1] At Aquinas College in Grand Rapids, Michigan, a separate "Emeritus College" was established to host seminars for retired people.[2] Boston University's "Evergreen Program" lets seniors audit any class for $15 each.[3]

In other countries there have also been model programs, stressing not only access for nontraditional students, but nontraditional methods as well. The Open University in Great Britain has been especially successful, as has the University of the Third Age throughout Europe.

Of course, the longstanding tradition of adult "folk education" in Scandinavia—which directly inspired Marty Knowlton—continues to this day.[4]

Perhaps the most notable of the educational initiatives designed specifically for elders is one that predates Elderhostel by more than a decade—the Institute Movement. Institutes, although varied in form and content, generally feature noncredit, college-level courses in the liberal arts and sciences. Like Elderhostel, the programs are usually located on the campuses of colleges or universities, but may also be found in libraries, YMCAs, museums, or other institutions with educational purposes. In contrast to Elderhostel's important travel aspect, however, Institutes involve older citizens in their home communities. The courses meet less frequently, but over a longer period of time than Elderhostel courses. The most distinctive feature of Institutes is that they are usually initiated, organized, and taught by elders themselves, thereby putting the older adult learner squarely in charge of his or her own educational future.

The first Institute was conceived at The New School for Social Research in New York City in 1962 by a number of retired school teachers. Dissatisfied with the unchallenging continuing education programs offered by their union, the teachers asked The New School if it would sponsor a more intellectually rigorous endeavor. Officials at The New School, known for its commitment to innovative education, were enthusiastic. They encouraged the teachers to form a self-governing group that would be responsible for managing courses taught by either New School faculty or by members of the teachers' group itself. The only requirement was that membership in classes be open to others than the original group.

The teachers agreed and a three-year experiment was launched as the Institute for Retired Professionals (IRP). There were two components to the program. The first feature of the IRP was the initiative enabling retired people to take regular New School courses. From an overwhelming 3,000 applicants, 404 members were selected. Paying $45 a year, they could enroll in any of The New School's regular daytime courses and use all of the School's facilities.[5]

The second component of the program, that which has come more commonly to be associated with the label "institute," was the weekly study groups which the retirees themselves organized and taught. Ranging in subject from French language to world affairs and literature, "these do-it-yourself courses [were] so successful that two of the Institute's student-instructors . . . joined the regular faculty of the New School."[6]

The program was immediately popular and soon there was a long waiting list of applicants for whom there was no room in the courses. Some sort of organization was clearly needed to manage this new program.

The late Hyman G. Hirsch, a member of the initial teachers' group, assumed the role of director of the Institute—at first an unpaid position. In this role, Hirsch guided the program through its formative years, helping it grow in both size and stature. In 1976 he convened a national conference at The New School focusing on the IRP, hoping to stimulate interest among other colleges and universities. The conference was a success, and soon IRP-modeled ventures began to flourish across the country.

The Institute for Learning in Retirement was founded at Syracuse University in 1975, at Harvard and Duke universities in 1977, and at American University in 1982; the Institute for Retired Professionals and Executives (IRPE), at Brooklyn College in 1977; the Academy of Lifelong Learning at the University of Delaware in 1980; and the PLATO Society (Perpetual Learning and Teaching Organization) at UCLA in 1980.* With these and many others, today there are over 100 Institute programs nationwide.

*The PLATO Society is one of sixteen Institutes on the West Coast that came together to form the Association for Learning in Retirement Organizations: West (ALIROW). The hope was that other regional groups would be formed. When this did not occur, the need became apparent for the Elderhostel Institute Network. ALIROW and the Network are closely associated in their work.

The initiative for creating an Institute normally comes from one or more interested local older adults. The initiating group, working in conjunction with the staff of the host institution:

> . . . transforms itself into a membership organization with bylaws and officers, and proceeds to develop an educational calendar and program and to recruit other members. In many cases, volunteer members make proposals to a curriculum committee of the membership and, utilizing a "peer teaching" mode, become the faculty of the Institute. In effect, the membership manages its own minicollege with the active support and encouragement of the host institution.*

Institute courses tend to resemble study groups more than traditional college classes. The emphasis is on older people teaching each other and group discussions prevail over one-sided lecturing. The erosion of the traditional distinction between the teacher as expert and students as learners is what makes the Institute's approach appealing to so many elders. Though in some cases the study group teacher is an emeritus faculty member with a lifetime of experience in the classroom, the group instructor is often a person with no formal teaching experience, who simply has a lively interest in a particular subject. For these self-taught teachers, the preparatory research is a labor of love, and it shows in the discussions they lead.

Bill Berkeley recalls meeting just such an Institute teacher, who had recently led a course on "The Film."

> This gentleman had been a hardware salesman all of his life, but did have an unusual interest in the movies. He described with a good deal of pride spending five solid months in the library educating himself on the history of the film industry. He shared with us the incredible high he had gotten when the "students" in his film course complimented him on the job that he had done in designing the course and leading the discussions. If you talk about older people seeking activities that will give them a feeling of dignity and self-worth, we can't think of anything that would fulfill those two requirements more than someone who has accomplished what our hardware salesman friend had done.

*This characterization is drawn from private study papers developed by the staff of Elderhostel in 1986.

As the above sketch indicates, Institute programs are not a place for passive individuals who expect to be spoon-fed information by a teacher. These elders are self-motivated, intellectually vital people who actively seek challenges. As Henry Lipman, former director of the Institute for Retired Professionals at The New School, put it, Institute programs "are for people who have in no way given up on themselves," people who are "not afraid of new ideas."

As gatherings of such dynamic, motivated elders, Institute programs often take on lives of their own, operating with the feel of bustling small towns. The Institute office is the center of a flurry of activity, serving a purpose akin to that of an old-time general store. The following description demonstrates that a well-functioning Institute program is, in the truest sense of the term, an intellectual community.

Every Tuesday morning thirty-five people gather in a college classroom to study the writings of John Steinbeck. Every person in the room is of retirement age. The leader is an emeritus faculty member of the college.

The students have prepared well. The learning process is lively, full of discussion, controversy, humor, disagreement, insight, and wisdom. When the class ends, the discussion continues in the halls, back to the office/lounge area, out to the parking lot.

This class is but one of twenty-five different study groups being offered by the Institute this semester. There are study groups meeting every day. Each meets once a week for two hours. There are no quizzes or grades—the study groups are noncredit. Most are led on a volunteer basis by members of the Institute; a few are taught by campus faculty. The typical member takes two study groups per semester.

The Institute juggles scheduling to occupy fully the two classrooms assigned for daytime use. These classrooms are down the hall from the office and lounge area that serves as the group's headquarters. The part-time director occupies an office that doubles as a committee meeting space. The full-time assistant's office has three desks; two are alternately used by committee chairpersons and members who provide clerical support.

A lively group of members shares rotating responsibility for maintaining the lounge (the coffee pot is ever brewing). A bulletin board carries announcements of a variety of Institute events: the monthly faculty lecture series, an upcoming concert by the Institute jazz combo, the annual spring membership meeting, the museum trip for the course on Impressionist art.

Participants in an ethics class at the Institute for Lifelong Education at Dartmouth listen to the instructor (above), and continue their discussion informally over lunch. (Photo courtesy of ILEAD)

About 300 of these lively over-sixty students have created this Institute. The Institute members pay dues, elect officers, and are largely self-governing in their efforts to provide exciting and stimulating educational experiences for themselves and their peers in the surrounding community.[7]

Like Elderhostelers, Institute participants often report that their personal and intellectual vitality has been restored by dynamic interaction with their peers. Florence Kassal of Florida International University's Elders Institute observed, the Institute "has given my mind a jump start to running knock-free and smoothly again. I found, along with my joints, it was becoming rusty."[8]

As Elderhostel and the Institute movement developed, it was obvious to all observers that there was substantial compatibility between the fundamental assumptions, values, goals, and clientele of the two programs. Both programs reject the view that aging is a process of failing energy and value, but rather affirm the continuing promise and dignity of older people. Both programs depend on the active, personal involvement of participants. Both programs assume that learning capacity does not decrease as years increase, but that in fact learning is a conducive means of self-fulfillment for elders.

However, Elderhostel and the Institutes did not develop at an equal pace. By the mid-1980s Elderhostel was growing at an astonishing rate of 20 to 30 percent per year, while the Institute program was expanding much more slowly. Furthermore, Elderhostel had established a balance between decentralized programming and a highly centralized national headquarters, but the Institute movement had no real center.

Leaders of various Institute programs had for a number of years sought a national mechanism to coordinate their efforts. The administration and Board of Directors of Elderhostel, equally aware of the programs' potential for mutual benefit, engaged in informal discussions with Institute officials. Finally, on June 12 and 13, 1986, the leaders convened a more formal meeting to consider "the desirability and feasibility of having Elderhostel serve as a *national coordinating organization* for the Institute movement."

As a result, on October 21, 1987, the Elderhostel Institute Network was established, giving Elderhostel official national coordinating responsibilities. The Elderhostel Institute Network represents a practical embodiment of the two programs' commonality of concern and their shared sense of commitment to elder education. From the Network's inception to the present, Elderhostel has made clear that it is coordinating and assisting the development of the Institute movement, not presuming in any way to direct or control it. The relationship is symbiotic and friendly.

The Network is guided formally by the Institute Network Advisory Committee, chaired by Henry Lipman, and on a day-to-day basis by Director James Verschueren.[9] An Elderhostel "original," Verschueren had been at Franconia College in 1975 when the first programs were offered. He then moved to New England College, where he coordinated over forty-five Elderhostel programs through 1983, when he became director of the New England Regional Elderhostel office.

Based at the New England Center for Continuing Education of the University of New Hampshire, Verschueren works with existing program leaders and also conducts workshops around the country to promote the development of new programs. The Network office publishes a newsletter, serves as an informational clearing house, provides technical assistance and facilitates program development, designs international programs for Institute members, and sponsors regional conferences of established Institutes.

Verschueren is an enthusiastic missionary, a promoter, and a believer in the power of people to help themselves. "These member-driven, learning communities," he says, "are like a light shining. The Institute idea has a lot of power. The fun part for me is to see people get excited about the idea and start recruiting people to help out."

Verschueren believes that one does not serve elders' educational needs by "doing things to them or even for them. We do have to help them take responsibility for their own lives." He admits, however, that "this is sometimes easier said than done. Older people have a lifetime of experience behind them and they know a very great deal about their needs and about how things are done."

Though they don't need to be done for, Verschueren feels that elders *do* need a programmatic framework to encourage them and engage them in learning. This is, of course, an institutional purpose shared by the Institute movement and Elderhostel. It is estimated that one-half of all Institute members are also on the Elderhostel mailing list. This substantial programmatic overlap reflects the commonality of values and concerns between the two programs. Verschueren stresses, however, that there are important differences:

The Elderhostel residential program is not an Institute-style approach to education. Those who are members of an Institute have a greater continuing personal investment in the program and share responsibility for the conduct of the educational activities. The movement helps us learn how to work with older people who are taking responsibility for their lives. In this sense Elderhostel can learn from the movement that it is facilitating.

Elders differ substantially, as do their personal circumstances. Some elders are not free to leave home and some cannot afford foreign travel, even at modest Elderhostel rates. For these people, there may be greater convenience in an Institute membership. Aside from these issues, many elders are more challenged by the opportunity to create, manage, or even teach in an Institute program than by the more traditional "student" role offered by Elderhostel residential programs. Being part of an Institute is an ongoing commitment, a membership in an active and continuous community. The adventures provided by Institute membership are exclusively intellectual and personal, without the physical and geographical adventures inherent in Elderhostel trips. In a sense, it's the difference between *visiting* a place and *living there*.

Although they are designed differently to meet somewhat different needs and clientele, Elderhostel and Institute programs are by all means complementary educational opportunities. In requiring participants to become actively engaged in learning, and to make an intellectual commitment that alters their priorities for living in later years, the programs assist elders in the movement from disengagement to liberation. The programs do not suggest that learning is easy or that the issues to be considered are simple or painless, but both take seriously Marty Knowlton's admonition, quoted in Chapter 2, that "this wasteful, tragic process of disengagement will continue unless older people themselves can realize their worth and become their own agents for change."

# CHAPTER FOURTEEN

# "THE STRANGE
# SUCCESS OF
# ELDERHOSTEL"

Reflecting on what the coming years may bring for elders in America, Marty Knowlton observed that "you don't have to be a futurist to see where we are heading. There will be more older people, living longer, in better health, and with the potential to make a creative contribution to society instead of just being dead weight. The big question concerns the quality of life. Will they be engaged and fully humane and will society have room for them on the national agenda?" For sixteen years, Marty and Elderhostel have been working hard to make the answer yes.

Elderhostel is but one initiative among many that reflect the growing numbers, new attitudes, economic force, and social awareness of elders. As opposed to the numerous lobbying and advocacy groups, Elderhostel as an educational organization has concentrated on meeting the personal needs of elders by providing opportunities for learning and self-fulfillment. In doing so, Elderhostel has expressed faith in a remarkably simple proposition: advanced age need not be a deterrent to continued learning, but rather can be the ideal context for educational and personal enrichment.

The only surprising or unusual thing about this simple proposition is that for so many years it received little recognition. As a society we have continually underestimated older people's potential and need for learning. Perhaps because we have so substantially tied education to youth and the development of vocation, we have considered education

somehow inappropriate or unnecessary for individuals who have retired. Whatever the reason, we have undervalued the importance of
learning and socialization in the lives of elders.

Arguing against this socially self-defeating practice, gerontology
writer Max Kaplan has suggested that liberal education—literally the
liberation of the mind for self-development—is the key to the reengage-
ment of elders in society. He writes:

The stereotypical myth that old people are useless, noncreative, sick, sexless,
conservative, and senile has . . . penetrated the universities in the administrative
halls as well as in the classrooms. The greater tragedy is that the mythology has
too often been accepted by the elderly themselves. It is just here that education
for them, and sometimes by them, provides the juices of confidence. The fight
against ageism must begin first in the minds of the elderly.[1]

Kaplan's statement reinforces the principles and strategies that have
guided the work of Elderhostel since its conception in 1974. Elderhostel
affirms the view that older people are capable of engagement rather
than disengagement, that they maintain a great capacity to think and
to talk and to care—and that all of these reasons provide the justifica-
tion for colleges and universities to direct some of their resources to the
educational needs of our growing older population.

Why would an institution wish to offer an Elderhostel program?
Certainly not to make money. Collecting only the modest tuition pay-
ment from each student (in 1991 it averaged $285 per program week, of
which $250 went to the participating institution), host institutions must
meet the instruction, food service, room, and staff costs required in
order to have a quality program. The programs are designed to be self-
supporting and most do break even, but some institutions participate
at a loss.

Elderhostel was originally proposed and supported at the University of New Hampshire in the context of a desire to utilize the space,
facilities, and human resources that were dormant during the summer
months. The concern to make maximum use of resources continues to
be a motivation for many host institutions. The more important motivations, however, are educational.

Elderhostel helps colleges and universities to fulfill their educational

Elderhostel group admires the architecture of the ancient Romans in Bath, England.

missions in a number of ways. First, by hosting an Elderhostel program, a college's doors are opened to a substantial new clientele.

The presence of an Elderhostel program on campus could be viewed as a cornerstone to a strategy to attract older learners to avail themselves of other educational opportunities. Because of the popularity and acceptance of Elderhostel by older people, it could serve as the basis for initially getting people on campus and introducing them to the educational system. Having alleviated some of the threats and fears associated with being a student through a successful Elderhostel experience, the older learner might be more favorably disposed to other educational programs and activities.[2]

Elderhostel's unique program design, which showcases liberal learning for its own sake, makes it an important part of any host institution's commitment to liberal education. At many institutions, faculty members so enjoy their Elderhostel teaching experiences that they put pressure on the administration to continue the program, even if it is not as profitable as the institution might wish. As a corollary motivation, institutions remain committed to Elderhostel because hostelers are so generally responsive. When the participants enjoy a program (which is overwhelmingly the case), everyone hears about it—not only the teachers and the campus coordinators, but the bus drivers, the kitchen staff, the maintenance people, and often the local newspaper. In these times of fierce institutional competition, the public relations boost is no small concern for administrators.

Furthermore, the mere presence of active elders can have a positive effect on campus. Kathleen O'Donnell points out that elders are among the most civically, socially, and politically involved citizens in America. "Involving these vibrant, active, aware men and women in campus life can have far-reaching positive effects on traditional students, faculty, administration, financial resources, graduate placement, and so on." [3]

Several years ago adult education specialist K. Patricia Cross directed her attention to "the strange success of Elderhostel." [4] She pointed out that by most indicators, Elderhostel *should* be a complete failure: survey data suggest that people over fifty-five are a poor market for educational programs; travel requirements are a barrier to the involvement of many elders; college courses taught by professors "rank near the bottom of all types of learning experiences described by older people"; and Elderhostel's cost, though low considering the program provided, is high by adult education standards. And yet, Elderhostel was obviously one of the most successful educational ventures to date.

In trying to explain this seemingly paradoxical success, Cross concluded that "an educational program is more than the sum of its parts. Elderhostel apparently offers an atmosphere of friendly conviviality with interesting people from all over the country, and it is the total experience rather than the classes per se that are the primary attraction." [5] This is a fine statement of the special magic that has characterized Elderhostel from the days of its founding. The "strange success of Elderhostel" derives its power from the total educational experience that is offered to older adults.

Elderhostel is a success story precisely because it has taken seriously the too-long overlooked hunger of older people to have lives of interest, challenge, and meaning. The organization has opened the educational door to hundreds of thousands of people who have known or suspected all along that the last phase of life can be a period of excitement and growth, rather than one of diminished meaning and withdrawal.

This is not to say that everyone who reaches the age of sixty or sixty-five is equally prepared to push forward into a new phase of growth or is hungry to learn. There are substantial differences among older adults, just as there are among people of twenty or forty. As has been discussed, those people who choose to participate in Elderhostel are very much a self-selecting group, unusually venturesome and risk-taking. There are many elders, even among those inclined toward education, for whom Elderhostel is not a comfortable fit.

It is possible, then, to acknowledge the great contributions Elderhostel has made to the lives of its participants without pretending that it is the be-all and end-all of adult education. Harry R. Moody has written:

Those who are comfortable coming to a college campus—Elderhostelers or IRP members—are typically well-educated people with positive prior experience with education. But campus-based learning is not for everyone. For other older people, access to higher education may have to come through the local senior center, or the church or synagogue, or perhaps even through store fronts or nursing homes.[6]

These options for older adult education need not be mutually exclusive or isolated from each other. As one very successful venture, Elderhostel has a responsibility to help foster other, more broad-based programs, to make late-life learning accessible to elders not among the self-selecting elite.

It is also important in discussing the success of Elderhostel not to pretend that it has solved the problems of aging. The good morale, self confidence, vitality, and positive view of life that are seen in so many Elderhostelers must be viewed against a background of poor morale and disengagement that is still the lot of millions of older people. It is difficult to say whether or not, in Marty Knowlton's words "society will have room for them on the national agenda."

The last two decades have produced a great many favorable developments for those whom the public has chosen to label as senior citizens. There have been health care victories, social security triumphs, age-discrimination protections, and improved retirement benefits. These policy changes have been accompanied by significant positive changes in prevailing attitudes toward elders. In fact, elders have received so much attention that some argue they get too much preferential treatment, such as discounted prices and allocation of so large a share of the federal budget. On occasion the press has reported a backlash against the elderly.[7]

It is certainly true that older Americans have found a voice for their interests and concerns. The AARP speaks on behalf of tens of millions of members and everybody from Congress to the media must listen. There is also the National Alliance of Senior Citizens, the National Council on Aging, Grey Panthers, and many additional special interest organizations that stand guard on behalf of elders. R. J. Havighurst has written that "the twentieth century has transformed the elderly from an almost invisible group sheltered by the extended family to a highly visible group with a life of its own, with moral and legal claims on society, and with a certain amount of political power."[8]

The future is far from certain, however. Currently almost one-third of the entire federal budget is devoted to benefits and programs supportive of elders, but there are still millions of older Americans who live marginally: poorly housed, improperly or insufficiently nourished, and without adequate health care. Furthermore, federal budget priorities are established from year to year, and priorities change over time. Although elders have been accorded an important position on the national agenda now, the degree of importance may fluctuate in years to come. The financial stresses of the recession during the early 1990s make clear that elders remain vulnerable.

The national agenda is not simply a matter of financial support. It is also a question of the attitudes of those in government and the general public. If the quality of life for elders is to improve, it can only be within a society that takes them seriously, understands and appreciates their abilities, and fully expects them to be contributing members of that society.

It is at precisely this point that Elderhostel has made its contributions in the past seventeen years. By their very nature, liberal and humane studies dignify and uplift the learner and challenge him or her to interact creatively with others and with society.[9] The unspoken agenda for each program is nothing less than the enrichment of the life and mind of the participant. The surprising success of the organization should not be such a surprise after all. When given the opportunity, most older people want to use their abilities and to remain thoughtful, informed members of the world in which they live.

By enrolling in an Elderhostel program or Institute, the participant is saying, in the words of one hosteler: "Don't count me out. I'm here and I intend to go on with my life by living it, not by buying into some notion that I no longer have the potential to become still better. I refuse to take seriously society's idea that at the arbitrary age of sixty-five I am suddenly a lamp going out."

What does the future hold for Elderhostel?

*Continued growth.* It would seem reasonably certain that demographic trends, along with ever-growing awareness of the program, will ensure a continuing expansion in the years ahead. In fact, as has been the case for most of Elderhostel's existence, the organization's greatest challenge will likely be the attempt to provide enough programming to meet the demand. If current rates of growth continue, there could be half a million participants a year by 1997.

Although host institutions have been flexible thus far in responding to Elderhostel's constant need for more courses and more space, competition for educational facilities is increasingly keen. If Elderhostel is to maintain the ability to grow, it will become more and more important to "sell" the program to educators and administrators.

*Expanding role.* Though Elderhostel has established relationships with a very large number of educational institutions, as of yet it has not become integral to the academic or public service lives of most of these institutions. This lack of integration has not resulted from any perceived failure of the program, but rather from its inherent design (relatively brief, noncredit courses for a constituency that soon departs from the campus), which tends to place the program at the periphery of institutional life.

There is an increasing interest, however, on the part of both Elderhostel and its affiliated educational institutions, to find ways in which the program can contribute more directly to institutional higher education. One way is for the Elderhostel experience to be documented and studied as the basis for research in the field of gerontology. As the authors of one study observe:

Because of the unique nature of the program and its success in attracting older adult students, a closer examination of the motives for attending Elderhostel... would not only increase our understanding of a particular subsample of the older adult learner population but provide valuable information that could be used by administrators and policy-makers in attracting older persons to their college programs.[10]

This investigative process has begun to a small but encouraging degree and a number of quite interesting papers have resulted.[11] The number of inquiries directed to the Boston office suggests that interest in the research opportunities afforded by Elderhostel is growing rapidly.

Elderhostel also has the potential to contribute to innovation in other aspects of higher education. The success of Elderhostel's and the Institutes' nontraditional approaches to teaching, curriculum, and course design may challenge current higher education policies and practices. Having discovered, for example, that older students fare better without credits, tests, and rigid student/teacher distinctions, educators might be led to reconsider the utility of these traditional practices in teaching students of all ages.

*Program innovation.* If the first seventeen years are any indication, it is likely that in the coming years Elderhostel's program design will take a number of new directions. These changes will not represent

Elderhostel cofounder David Bianco (left) and author Eugene Mills (center) review management issues with Bill Berkeley during a visit to the Elderhostel office in Boston.

any fundamental break with the past, but rather elaborations of the core concept (just as year-long programming, international courses and intensive-study units were, at their initiation, "new directions").

Innovations in program location have already begun. The list of host institutions, at first exclusively college campuses, has expanded to include a variety of educational and outdoors centers and parks. Program Director Judy Goggin foresees a continuation of this trend, with new partnerships forged between Elderhostel and museums and other specialized institutions. Another recent innovation is recreational-vehicle programming, in which participants drive from site to site in their own RVs. As an elaboration of this idea, Goggin hopes to develop other "moving" courses, such as one in which participants would retrace a pioneer trail, learning geography and period history along the way.

In terms of program content, a number of brand-new ideas will be pursued in coming years. Theme programs, in which all three courses relate to one broader subject—for example, fine arts, music, marine studies, or writing and sexuality—will continue to be an appealing option for many hostelers, as will intensive study units. Program co-ordinators will look for more ways to integrate the curriculum and make the Elderhostel unit a more cohesive experience.

Other new directions include intergenerational courses, which hostelers attend with their children or grandchildren. Some participants have suggested that Elderhostel sponsor Peace Corps-like programs for elders, international and/or domestic internship opportunities in critical settings such as hospitals, housing projects, marine research centers, or museums.

Though there have been changes through the years and there will continue to be experiments with new approaches, Elderhostel holds fast to what works: the original program design. There would appear to be an exquisite rightness about one week, three courses, no tests, and a mix of extracurricular activities. As Bill Berkeley puts it:

> . . . the genius of the idea and the genius of Marty Knowlton was not only in coming up with an overall concept which acknowledged the new breed of older person before most everybody else did, but in the particulars of the design of the program. He came up with a model that seems to serve lots of different components of the older adult population, lots of different kinds of curricula and is adaptable to an incredible variety of institutions.

Without the creative dream and unflinching persistence of Marty Knowlton and David Bianco, Elderhostel never would have happened. Their energetic—at times frantic—leadership assured the early spread of the program and, in the case of Knowlton, has been a continuing force for the organization's growth and vitality.[*]

Organizations that have a charismatic beginning often lose the

---

[*]Though continuing a personal involvement in Elderhostel, recently Marty has launched a new program, Gatekeepers to the Future. This initiative focuses on the need for an organization that speaks on behalf of unborn generations. He says, "Someone has to speak for the group of people who cannot yet speak for themselves."

David Bianco has been relatively less involved in Elderhostel since he left the University of New Hampshire in 1979. Subsequently, he served as manager of Thompson Island Education Center in Boston Harbor and more recently he has been general manager of Boston's Longwood Cricket Club.

power, flexibility, and creativity that characterized their early years. The realities of administration and the need to be cautious in order to assure the continuation of the organization lead to what Max Weber called "the routinization of charisma." The story of Elderhostel reveals such a transformation, but in this case the organization has remained remarkably flexible and creative. From the encouragement of Elderhostel Canada, to the development of the Institute Network, to the continuing reexamination of program location and curriculum, Elderhostel is an ever-experimenting, ever-changing, energetic organization.

Another common pitfall of organizations initially focused on a single charismatic figure is that they act like sparklers on the Fourth of July: burning brightly while the leader is an energetic presence, then fizzling rapidly when he or she moves away. Elderhostel's fortunate avoidance of this phenomenon can be attributed to the thoughtful and professional leadership of Bill Berkeley and Mike Zoob, who guided the organization through the crucial transition period and continue to serve as devoted administrators. They have been able to work with Marty Knowlton to forge a comfortable balance between managing success and keeping alive the spirit of the enterprise. There have been tensions, of course, but for the most part these have been creative tensions.

The success of Elderhostel is not only a tribute to the soundness of the original idea, the foresight of its founders, and the creative energy of those who administered and taught in the programs. It is also an indication of how ready America was for an educational program that took seriously the individual's capacity for late-life learning. Such a program was long overdue in 1975, and the need for it is all the more apparent now after seventeen years of service. As long as there are elders who have the desire to learn and to continue growing—*in other words, as long as there are elders*—there will be a place and a need for Elderhostel. The program is a dignified, constructive response to aging which affords elders the opportunity to expand their horizons, have fun, and find a place to belong. One participant speaks for many in saying "Every time I go to an Elderhostel week I think, 'this is where I want to be.'"

Judging by the sentiment of this hosteler and the hundreds of thousands of elders like her who have ventured on the hosteling experience, there may be a significant amount of truth in the remark Judy Goggin once heard at a conference: "There are only three things to look forward to in getting older: Social Security, Medicare, and Elderhostel."

Hands-on computer class at Western New England College in Massachusetts.

# ELDERHOSTEL

# BOARD OF

# DIRECTORS (as of March 4, 1992)

| *Name* | *Title/Location* |
|---|---|
| David W. Ellis<br>*Chairman* | President and Director, Museum of<br>   Science<br>Boston, Massachusetts |
| Harry R. Moody<br>*Vice Chairman* | Deputy Director<br>Brookdale Center on Aging of Hunter<br>   College<br>New York, New York |
| Ragan A. Henry<br>*Treasurer* | Partner<br>Wolf, Block Schorr & Solis-Cohen<br>Philadelphia, Pennsylvania |
| Willard L. Boyd | President, Field Museum of Natural<br>   History<br>Chicago, Illinois |
| Merrell M. Clark | President, Elderworks<br>Scarsdale, New York |
| James F. English, Jr. | President Emeritus, Trinity College<br>West Hartford, Connecticut |
| E. Margaret Fulton | Education Consultant<br>Vancouver, British Columbia, Canada |
| Charles F. C. Henderson | Elderhosteler and Retired Teacher<br>Needham, Massachusetts |
| Martin P. Knowlton | Founder, Elderhostel<br>Sausalito, California |

Henry Lipman

Elderhosteler
and Former Director, Institute of
Retired Professionals
New York, New York

Eugene S. Mills

President Emeritus, Whittier College
and Former President, University of
New Hampshire
Durham, New Hampshire

David A. Peterson

Director, Leonard Davis School of
Gerontology, Ethel Percy Andrus
Gerontology Center
University of Southern California
Los Angeles, California

Walter Pitman

Elderhosteler and Educator
Toronto, Ontario, Canada

Beverly Shaver

Elderhosteler and Travel Writer
El Cerrito, California

*Representing Elderhostel Canada*
Robert Williston

Executive Director, Elderhostel Canada
Kingston, Ontario, Canada

*Ex-officio*
Alice Brown

State Director, Kentucky Elderhostel
University of Kentucky
Lexington, Kentucky

Cynthia Giguere

Regional Director, New England
Elderhostel
University of New Hampshire
Durham, New Hampshire

Marcia Schekel

State Director, Washington Elderhostel
Washington State University
Pullman, Washington

*Founding Chairman Emeritus*
Charles E. Odell, Sr.

Former Chairman
Pinehurst, North Carolina

# Elderhostel Board of Directors

*Founding Directors*

Mildred McAfee Horton — Former President, Wellesley College
Wellesley, Massachusetts

Frank J. Manning
(deceased) — President
Massachusetts Association of Older
   Americans

Ollie Randall
(deceased) — Founder, Gerontology Society
   and Founder, National Council on
   Aging

May Sarton — Writer
York, Maine

# NOTES

## Introduction

1. Jerome L. Avorn, "Medicine: The Life and Death of Oliver Shay," in *Our Aging Society: Paradox and Promise*, Alan Pifer and Linda Bronte, eds. (New York: W. W. Norton & Company, 1986), 283.

2. Robert N. Butler, *Why Survive? Being Old in America* (New York: Harper & Row, 1975), 404.

3. From "Elderhostel," a 1976 paper reviewing the establishment of the organization.

4. Harry R. Moody, *Abundance of Life: Human Development Policies for an Aging Society* (New York: Columbia University Press, 1988), 205.

## 2. The Vision

1. David Bianco and Martin P. Knowlton, "A Proposal: An Institute of International Life at Boston University," *Journal of Education*, vol. 152 (1969) 35.

2. Ibid. 40.

3. Elderhostel Catalog, any issue, 2.

## 3. The First Summer

1. Ellie McRath, "They Call the Teacher 'Sonny,'" *Time* (July 23, 1984), 89.

2. John McAllister, "Network of 'ElderHostels' to Open in State," *Portsmouth Herald* (Apr. 7, 1975).

3. "Five Colleges Operate Elderly Hostels," *Portsmouth Herald* (Aug. 4, 1975).

4. Sterne Barnett, "Elderhostel '75," *Pictorial Living Coloroto Magazine* (Oct. 12, 1975), 44.

5. "20 New England Colleges Give Summer Programs for Elderly," *New York Times* (Nov. 16, 1975), 69.

6. Barnett, "Elderhostel '75," 44.

### 4. Unsolicited Generosity

1. Betty Holroyd Roberts, "A Report Evaluating the Effectiveness of Elderhostel '75," 15.
2. "Elderhostel '76: A Summary Statement," 28.
3. Ibid. 23–24.

### 5. Instant Momentum

1. Eleanor Gurewitsh, "Elderhostel: A Good Idea is Growing and Growing," *Aging* (Jan./Feb. 1980), 14.
2. From a written summary of reminiscences by William Berkeley, 1989, p. 4.
3. Berkeley, summary of reminiscences, p. 6.
4. Gurewitsh, "Elderhostel," 14.

### 6. A Cause for Celebration

1. From a written summary of reminiscences by William Berkeley, 1989, pp. 7–8.
2. Max Kaplan, "Elderhostel: Using a Lifetime of Learning and Experience," *Change* (Jan./Feb. 1981), 41.

### 7. The 1980s

1. In 1990–1991, 20 percent of that year's participants contributed to the Fund; of Elderhostel's entire mailing list, 17 percent contributed.
2. Boston office, "History and Format of Elderhostel International Programs," 1987, 1.
3. Ibid., 2.
4. Elderhostel International Catalog, Winter/Spring 1992, 4.
5. Walter Pitman, "Reaching Out to the Mature Learner—A New Direction for Canadian Universities," *Canadian Journal of Higher Education IV* (1974), 75–80.

### 8. Elderhostel Today

1. *Between Classes*, vol. 4, no. 3 (1987), 1.

### 12. Elders in America

1. *Statistical Abstract of the United States*, (Washington, D.C.: Bureau of the Census, 1990), 445–60. It should be added that the median income for those *over* sixty-five was only $14,334.
2. Fabrian Linden, "The $800 Billion Market," *American Demographics* (Feb. 1986), 4–6.
3. See A. H. Maslow, *Motivation and Personality* (New York: Harper & Row, 1954).

4. David B. Wolfe, *Serving the Ageless Market* (New York: McGraw Hill, Inc., 1990), 100–32.

5. John McLeish, *The Ulyssean Adult* (Toronto: McGraw-Hill Reyerson, 1976), 309.

6. Joanna Walker, "Older People as Consumers of Education: The Politics of Provision and Participation," in *Educational Gerontology: International Perspectives*, Frank Glendenning, ed. (New York: St. Martin's, 1985), 206.

7. *1990 Digest of Educational Statistics* (Washington, D.C.: National Center for Educational Statistics, 1991), Table 160.

8. Kathleen M. O'Donnell, "Older Learners: A Viable Clientele," in *New Directions for Higher Education*, no. 29 (San Francisco: Jossey-Bass, 1980), 73.

9. *Statistical Abstract* (1990), 134.

10. Moody, *Abundance of Life*, 194.

11. K. Patricia Cross, *Adults as Learners: Increasing Participation and Facilitating Learning* (San Francisco: Jossey-Bass, 1982), 222.

12. Victor M. Agruso, Jr., *Learning in the Later Years: Principles of Educational Gerontology* (New York: Academic Press, 1978), 128.

13. See Cross, *Adults as Learners*, 98.

14. Moody, *Abundance of Life*, 203.

15. H. R. Moody, "What Can We Learn From Elderhostel?" (A private paper provided the author by Moody), Jan., 1990, 2.

16. Dorothy Townsend, "Elderhostel—Learning Can Begin at 60." *Los Angeles Times* (Aug. 20, 1978), 1.

17. According to the 1990 *Statistical Abstract of the United States* (Table 42), 10.2 percent of Americans sixty-five and older had attended one to three years of college and 10.6 percent had four years or more.

18. In a 1989 survey of American and Canadian participants, 2.7 percent reported an annual income under $10,000, 11.8 percent $10,000 to $19,999, and 22.8 percent $20,000 to $29,999.

19. See Cady Goldfield, "Elderhostel: Providing Learning Opportunities for Active Seniors," *National Bar Association Magazine* (June 1990), 34–36.

## *13. Elders Teaching Elders*

1. David A. Peterson, "The Development of Education for Older People in the USA," in *Educational Gerontology: International Perspectives*; Frank Glendenning, ed. (New York: St. Martin's, 1985, p. 88.

2. Northrop J. Hruby, "Emeritus College: Reaching the Older Learner," in *New Directions for Higher Education*, no. 29 (San Francisco: Jossey-Bass, 1980), 87–95.

3. Melinda Beck, "School Days for Seniors," *Newsweek* (Nov. 11, 1991), 60.

4. See Ragnar Lund, ed, *Scandinavian Adult Education* (Copenhagen: Det danske Forlag, 1952).

5. "Senior Scholars," *Newsweek* (Jan. 20, 1964), 77.

6. Ibid.

7. From "The Institute Movement and Elderhostel: A National Overview," prepared by the Elderhostel Institute Network, Nov. 7, 1991, p. 1.

8. As quoted in the Elders Institute Fall Schedule of Courses of Florida International University (Oct. 1989), p. 8.

9. Other members of the committee at the time of writing are Sara Craven, director of the Duke Institute for Learning in Retirement; James F. English, member of the Elderhostel Board of Directors and president emeritus of Trinity College, Hartford, Connecticut; John W. Hollenbach, executive secretary of the Academy of Senior Professionals, Hope College, Michigan; Francis Meyers, president of the Association of Learning in Retirement Organizations, West; Sally Noble, director of Wyoming Elderhostel; Ruth Paine, member ElderCollege, University of Nevada, Reno, Nevada; Nancy Sack, vice-chair and member of the Harvard Institute for Learning in Retirement; M. Elizabeth Scott, member of the Renaissance Institute, College of Notre Dame of Maryland; and Kenneth Young, former director of the Institute for Learning in Retirement, American University, Washington, D.C.

## 14. *"The Strange Success of Elderhostel"*

1. Max Kaplan, "Elderhostel: Using a Lifetime of Experience," *Change* (Jan./Feb. 1981), 41.

2. Jean Romaniuk and Michael Romaniuk, "Participation Motives of Older Adults in Higher Education," *The Gerontologist*, vol. 22 (1982), 368.

3. O'Donnell, "Older Learners," 72.

4. K. Patricia Cross, "The State of the Art in Needs Assessments," *Community Junior College*, no. 7 (1983), 195–206.

5. Ibid., 204.

6. Moody, *Abundance of Life*, 207.

7. For a discussion of this "inter-generational issue," see Ken Dychtwald, *Age Wave* (Los Angeles: Jeremy P. Tarcher, Inc., 1989), 63–66.

8. Quoted in Frank Glendenning, ed., "The Aging Society," in *Educational Gerontology: International Perspectives* (New York: St. Martin's, 1985), 24.

9. This theme was considered early in the history of Elderhostel. See Martin P. Knowlton, "Liberal Arts: The Elderhostel Plan for Survival," *Educational Gerontology*, no. 2 (1977), 87–93.

10. Romaniuk and Romaniuk, "Participation Motives," 365.

11. Among others: Romaniuk and Romaniuk, *op. cit.*; Michael Brady and Mary Lee Fowler, "Participation Motives and Learning Outcomes Among Older Learners," *Educational Gerontology*, vol. 14, no. 1 (1988), 45–56; Michael Brady, "Personal Growth and the Elderhostel Experience," *Lifelong Learning* vol. 7, no. 3 (1983), 11–13.

# INDEX

UNIVERSITY PRESS OF NEW ENGLAND publishes books under its own imprint and is the publisher for Brandeis University Press, Brown University Press, University of Connecticut, Dartmouth College, Middlebury College Press, University of New Hampshire, University of Rhode Island, Tufts University, University of Vermont, and Wesleyan University Press.

Library of Congress Cataloging-in-Publication Data

Mills, Eugene S.
　The story of Elderhostel / Eugene S. Mills ; foreword by Rosalynn Carter.
　p.　cm.
　ISBN 0–87451–599–8. — ISBN 0–87451–600–5 (pbk.)
　1. Elderhostels—History.　2. Elderhostels—United States—History.　I. Title.
LC5457.M55　1993
374'.01—dc20　　　92–53864